The Zucchini Cookbook

The Zucchini Cookbook

by Paula Simmons

THIRD EDITION,
REVISED & ENLARGED

Pacific Search Press

Pacific Search Press, 222 Dexter Avenue North,
    Seattle, Washington 98109
©1983 by Pacific Search Press. All rights reserved
Printed in the United States of America

First edition published in 1974
Second edition published in 1975

Second printing 1986

Designed by Judy Petry

Library of Congress Cataloging in Publication Data

Simmons, Paula.
    The zucchini cookbook.

    Includes index.
    1. Cookery (Zucchini) I. Title.
TX803.Z82S55   1983   641.6'562   83-8591
ISBN 0-914718-81-9 (pbk.)

Contents

On the Vine

As it was for millions of other Americans, this past decade may well have been a time when you rediscovered your garden or joined others at a city garden plot, composted, planted, and found yourself with a vegetable bounty at harvest time—one that most likely included an unwieldy bumper crop of zucchini. Perhaps you were one of the few who knew of more ways to prepare this summer squash than just sauteing it and simmering it in an Italian tomato sauce. More likely, however, you were on the lookout for recipes as delicious and diverse as those Paula Simmons offered in her first edition of *The Zucchini Cookbook*, published in 1974.

If you were in the lucky throng of book buyers who discovered this treasure, the challenge of the mighty zucchini was eased considerably. What has made this guide to preparing the zucchini a classic? Surely the kitchen counters filled with aromatic zucchini breads and cakes, zucchini quiches, zucchini lasagna, even zucchini ice creams, are the key. More than 150,000 copies of *The Zucchini Cookbook* have wended their way into the cookbook collections of a nation, testimony to Paula Simmons's way with a squash.

To celebrate the success of her book and to pay homage to the hardy, prolific vines that bear the zucchini, Paula has collected thirty-four new kitchen-tested recipes for this enlarged third edition of *The Zucchini Cookbook*. This is no mean feat if you consider that Paula Simmons is also busy employing her eight additional arms and hands in the business of raising sheep for handspun yarn, weaving on commission, giving spinning workshops across the country, writing new books, and tending her garden. What she calls her "casual cooking" has become synonymous with good food.

As always, Paula combines down-home cuisine—Corn and Zucchini Pie, Cheese Steaks with Zucchini and Sour Cream, and Zucchini-Filled Potato Roll—with international dishes like India Fried Zucchini, Hot Dutch Vegetable Salad, and Green Zucchini Enchilada Sauce. Just as there is no need to coax the zucchini to materialize from the lovely yellow blossoms on the vine (they will simply burst upon the garden mounds en masse), there will be no need for you to coax one or two good recipes from the pages of *The Zucchini Cookbook*. They, too, will startle and delight you with their numbers, their variety, and their goodness.

Pacific Search Press

Grow It

The zucchini is a very fast growing, prolific variety of summer squash. Since it is a compact, bushy plant, it is convenient for home gardeners. Its huge leaves make it highly ornamental but tend to hide some of the green fruits, so that even with daily inspection some squash will escape detection and grow to monster size. Ideally, they should be picked when immature; leaving too many to grow to huge sizes can slow down the blooming and production of new fruit. But there are some recipes for the escapees.

For an early crop, plant seeds indoors in compressed peat pots a few weeks before the average date of the last frost. Set the plants into the garden as soon as all danger of frost is past. When plants have their second set of leaves, if the weather is still too cool at night, you can either set them out and provide protection or transplant to a gallon can with drainage holes in the bottom. Set the can outside during the day and bring it in at night. Keep these small plants well watered, for low indoor humidity dries them out quickly.

For seeding directly into the soil, wait until danger of frost is past, then sow in hills or rows with well-rotted manure buried below them, five seeds to a hill, in hills four feet apart from center to center. These can be thinned to the strongest two or three plants. When plants are well established, a heavy straw mulch around them will keep down the weeds and conserve moisture. Zucchini need a lot of water at the roots, but not on the crown of the plant or on the immature fruits. If the soil is poor and water tends to run off instead of soak in, make a trench-and-dike arrangement for watering or sink a large can with lots of drainage holes in the bottom next to the squash plants while they are small. Fill the can with water and it will slowly drain into the soil by the squash roots.

Most zucchini varieties take only 40 to 55 days for the first little squash to be ready to eat. (Winter squash, by comparison, take from 100 to 125 days.) The fruits develop from the bright yellow female blossoms, which are low on short stems. These are pollinated from the yellow male blossoms, which are on long upright stems. It is estimated that three hills of zucchini will amply supply a family of four if you keep the fruits picked to encourage more bearing. Zucchini will keep for several days in the refrigerator. At the end of the season let a few grow to monster size; pick them and store in a cool place as you would winter squash and the zucchini will keep until December.

There are many good varieties available, but we were particularly impressed with the new hybrid Aristocrat zucchini, a 1973 "All American" winner. It is quick to mature, with first fruits ready within 48 days of sowing seed directly into the garden, and is very prolific with a good keeping quality. Developed by the Peto Seed Company in California, it is available from

W. Atlee Burpee Company and a number of other sources. The new Burpee Golden zucchini is worth some garden space for its attractive bright yellow color, but it is no match for the Aristocrat in either taste or production. Beautini from Jung Seed Company and Elite from Harris Seed Company are two other early hybrids that are more satisfactory. And for fun and a conversation piece, Nichols Garden Nursery has seeds for two tasty novelties—a round zucchini shaped like a small cantaloupe, and Courese, a white one from France which is firm-meated with very few seeds.

For a plentiful supply of zucchini in spring, summer, and fall, GROW IT!

And Cook It!

WHAT CAN I DO WITH A BIG ZUCCHINI? A common lament of home gardeners and their friends. This book has dozens of answers. Many recipes are created especially for the king-size zucchini, the one that remains hidden under those beautiful big squash leaves until it seems much too huge for cooking, valuable only as a conversation piece.

HOW CAN I GET MY CHILDREN TO EAT VEGETABLES? The blues song of mothers everywhere. They don't like zucchini? Perhaps they don't like the way it is prepared. Try irresistible chocolate zucchini cake, pineapple zucchini cookies, zucchalmond squares, zucchini tacos, zucchini a la maddalena, swiss steak with invisible zucchini, cream of zucchini soup, zucchini dill pickles, or some old favorites like the popular zucchini breads. If you think it can only be served boiled with salt and pepper, try *The Zucchini Cookbook.*

My cooking instructions are sometimes casual. Baking measurements are always given for unsifted flour, and dry ingredients are usually just mixed instead of sifted together. In all my recipes this seems to work just fine. The cake recipes are very easy. Most need no frosting and are cut-in-the-pan cakes that offer the appeal of cake with the convenience of bar cookies.

Some recipes suggest a Teflon utensil because less liquid is required when using a nonstick finish and less oil is needed to saute, fry, or brown food. My own use of nonstick skillets started with an aversion to pot scrubbing. If you are not using Teflon, you may need to add a trifle more liquid or fat to some recipes, and stir a bit more, too.

I often say "steam" the zucchini. If you don't have a vegetable steamer (a little perforated basket on legs that fits inside any saucepan with a lid), it is a worthwhile investment, a versatile kitchen helper, and useful for many other vegetables when liquid will not be used as part of the recipe.

A note on calories of some cooked vegetables:

calories per pound

Zucchini	74
Cabbage	109
Spinach	115
Carrots	138
Beets	187
Peas	300-400

depending on maturity

Breads,
Dips, and Spreads

Zucchini Yeast Bread

Flour   8 to 9 cups
Active dry yeast   2 packets
Sugar   ¾ cup
Salt   1 tablespoon
Wheat germ   ¾ cup
Zucchini milk (see Index)   1½ cups
Water   ½ cup
Margarine   ¾ cup
Eggs   4

In large mixer bowl, combine 3 cups flour, yeast, sugar, salt, and wheat germ; mix well. In saucepan, heat zucchini milk, water, and margarine until just warm. Add with eggs to flour mixture. Blend at low speed; beat 3 minutes at medium speed. By hand, gradually stir in enough flour to make a firm dough. Knead on floured surface until smooth, 5 to 8 minutes. Place in greased bowl; turn to grease top. Cover and let rise in warm place until doubled, about 1 to 1½ hours. Punch dough down. Divide into 3 parts and shape into loaves. Place in greased 8 × 4-inch pans. Cover and let rise in warm place until doubled, about 45 minutes. Bake at 375° for 25 to 30 minutes, until golden brown. Remove from pans, brush tops of loaves with oil, and cool on wire rack. Makes 3 loaves.

Light Zucchini Bread

Eggs   3
Vegetable oil   ¾ cup
Sugar   1½ cups
Powdered lemon peel   1 teaspoon
Orange extract   ½ teaspoon
Vanilla   ¼ teaspoon
Zucchini   2 cups grated (can be firm flesh of very large one, peeled if
     peeling is tough)
Flour   2½ cups (or more*)
Salt   ¾ teaspoon
Cinnamon   ½ teaspoon
Ginger   ¼ teaspoon
Soda   1 teaspoon
Baking powder   2 teaspoons
Nuts   ½ cup chopped

Beat eggs; add oil and sugar; beat well. Add flavoring and zucchini; beat. Mix dry ingredients together; stir in and add nuts; mix well. Bake in small loaf pans or in oiled cans (size #2½) at 350° for 1 hour. Cool in cans until bread will remove easily, then cool on wire rack. This freezes well and is an ideal way to use up those monsters.

* You may need more flour if using small- or medium-size zucchini that have more moisture. If using very large zucchini, discard the center pulp. The firm flesh is not extra moist, but perfect for this recipe.

Dark Zucchini Bread

Eggs 3
Vegetable oil 1 cup
Brown sugar 2 cups firmly packed
Vanilla 3 teaspoons
Zucchini 3 cups grated (can be firm flesh of very large one, peeled if
     peeling is tough)
Molasses 1 tablespoon
Flour 4 cups
Salt 1 teaspoon
Soda 1 teaspoon
Baking powder ¼ teaspoon
Cinnamon 2 teaspoons
Pumpkin pie spice 1 teaspoon
Nuts ½ cup chopped

Beat eggs; add oil and brown sugar; beat well. Add vanilla, grated zucchini, and molasses; beat. Mix dry ingredients together; add nuts and beat well. Bake in greased and floured small loaf pans or in 3 oiled cans (size #2½) at 350° for 1 hour. Cool in cans until bread will remove easily, then cool on rack.
Note: This freezes well. To freeze in cans, cool bread completely, then return it to can; top with double layer of foil tied securely over top of can.

Chocolate Zucchini Bread

Eggs 3
Vegetable oil 1 cup
Brown sugar 2 cups firmly packed
Vanilla 1 teaspoon
Zucchini 3 cups grated (can be firm flesh of very large one, peeled if peeling is tough)
Baker's unsweetened chocolate 2 squares, melted
Flour 4 cups
Salt 1 teaspoon
Soda 1 teaspoon
Baking powder ¼ teaspoon
Cinnamon 1 teaspoon
Pumpkin pie spice 1 teaspoon
Nuts ½ cup chopped

Beat eggs; add oil and brown sugar; beat well. Add vanilla, zucchini, and chocolate; beat. Mix dry ingredients together; add nuts and beat well. Bake in 6 tiny greased loaf pans, or in 2 standard loaf pans at 350° for 40 to 60 minutes, depending on loaf size. Cool in pans until bread will remove easily, then cool on rack.

Bran Bread

Flour 2 cups
Baking powder 2 teaspoons
Salt ½ teaspoon
Soda ½ teaspoon
Sugar ⅓ cup
Allspice ¾ teaspoon
Bran flakes 1 cup
Nuts ½ cup chopped
Egg 1, beaten
Buttermilk 1¼ cups
Shortening 3 tablespoons, melted
Zucchini 1 cup diced (can be from large one)

Mix together flour, baking powder, salt, soda, sugar, and allspice; add bran flakes and nuts. Combine egg with buttermilk and melted shortening; add to dry ingredients and beat just enough to mix well. Stir in zucchini. Bake in greased and floured 9 × 5 × 3-inch loaf pan at 350° approximately 50 to 60 minutes. A very moist bread; cuts best when cool.

Zucchini Kuchen

Egg 1, plus water to make ⅔ cup
Onion 2 tablespoons grated
Biscuit mix 2¼ cups
Zucchini 1 medium
Mayonnaise
Poppy seeds

Break egg into measuring cup and add water to fill to ⅔ cup mark. Add this to onion and biscuit mix; stir with fork. Turn out, knead lightly, and pat into oiled 9-inch round pan. Slice zucchini in ⅛-inch rounds; arrange slices overlapping on top of dough. Spread tops thickly with mayonnaise. Sprinkle with poppy seeds. Bake at 425° for 25 to 30 minutes. Serves 6.

Any leftovers can be reheated in foil and are just as tasty.

Pancakes

Egg 1
Flour ½ cup
Salt ⅛ teaspoon
Sugar 1 teaspoon
Zucchini 1 cup grated (can be from large one)

Beat egg well. Mix flour, salt, and sugar together; sift over zucchini and fold this into the egg. Drop from tablespoon on greased griddle; flatten with back of spoon. Cook until golden brown; turn and brown other side. Cook until done through. Good with honey or syrup.

Date Bran Muffins

All-Bran cereal 1 cup
Milk 5 tablespoons
Eggs 2
Cooking oil ½ cup
Zucchini 2 cups shredded
Flour 1½ cups
Baking powder 3 teaspoons
Salt ⅛ teaspoon
Sugar 4 tablespoons
Cinnamon ⅛ teaspoon
Dates ¾ cup chopped

Combine cereal and milk; let stand 15 minutes to soften. Add eggs, oil, and zucchini; mix well. Mix dry ingredients and stir in until just moistened. Stir in dates. Fill muffin tins ½ full. Bake about 20 minutes at 400°. Makes 18 large muffins.

Muffins

Flour 2 cups
Salt ¾ teaspoon
Baking powder 2 teaspoons
Sugar 3 tablespoons
Mace ⅛ teaspoon ground
Butter or margarine 2 tablespoons
Zucchini 1 cup finely chopped
Egg 1
Milk ½ cup
Cinnamon ½ teaspoon
Sugar 1 tablespoon

Mix flour, salt, baking powder, sugar, and mace. Cut in butter with pastry blender or fork. Add zucchini; mix. Add egg beaten lightly with milk. Spoon into greased muffin tins. Mix cinnamon and sugar and sprinkle on top of muffin batter. Bake at 400° approximately 20 minutes.

Cracker Toppers or Dips

Variation 1

Chili sauce ¼ cup
Mayonnaise ¼ cup
Prepared horseradish 1 tablespoon
Zucchini ½ cup chopped

Mix and chill.

Variation 2

Deviled ham spread 1 2¼-ounce can
Prepared mustard 1 teaspoon
Worcestershire sauce 1 teaspoon
Zucchini ½ cup shredded and drained

Mix and chill.

Variation 3

Sharp cheese 1 cup shredded
Zucchini 1 cup finely chopped
Walnuts ½ cup chopped
Mayonnaise ¾ cup

Mix and chill.

Variation 4

Margarine ½ cup, softened
Zucchini 3 tablespoons chopped
Carrot 1 tablespoon grated
Celery 1 tablespoon finely chopped
Green pepper 1 tablespoon chopped
Seasoned salt 1 teaspoon

Mix and chill.

Variation 5

Sharp cheese   sliced and cut in squares
Dill pickles   sliced crossways
Zucchini   small, sliced crossways

Top crackers with slice of pickle, slice of zucchini, and slice of cheese; broil until cheese melts.

Variation 6

Several small zucchini, centers removed with apple corer. Stuff with mixture of:

Cream cheese   4 ounces, softened
Bacon   2 slices, crumbled
Garlic salt   to taste

Chill. Slice crossways and serve on crackers spread with mayonnaise.

Variation 7

Onion   1 tablespoon chopped
Zucchini   1 cup chopped
Tomato sauce   ⅔ cup
Hot pepper sauce   5 drops
Cream cheese   4 ounces, cut in chunks
Dill pickle   1, finely chopped

Simmer onion, zucchini, tomato sauce, and hot pepper sauce for 15 to 20 minutes. Put in blender container with cream cheese; blend until very smooth. Stir in chopped dill pickle. Chill until ready to serve.

Variation 8

Zucchini   1 cup grated (can be firm flesh of large one)
Plain yogurt   3 tablespoons
Seasoned salt   ¼ teaspoon
Garlic powder   ¼ teaspoon
Freeze-dried shallots   1 teaspoon (or ½ teaspoon chopped fresh shallots)
Paprika   to garnish

Drain zucchini in colander. Press between towels to drain off more liquid. Combine with yogurt, seasonings, and shallots. Garnish with a sprinkle of paprika. Chill well.

Cakes,
Cookies, and Desserts

Lemony Zucchini Cake

Sugar   ¾ cup
Flour   1¼ cups
Baking powder   2 teaspoons
Salt   ⅛ teaspoon
Powdered lemon peel   1 teaspoon
Milk   ½ cup
Egg   1
Honey   ½ cup
Vanilla   ½ teaspoon
Lemon extract   ½ teaspoon
Zucchini   ¾ cup finely chopped (not grated)

Stir together dry ingredients in large bowl. Add rest of ingredients, except zucchini. Beat well, about 5 minutes. Stir in zucchini. Bake in greased and floured 9 × 9-inch pan about 35 minutes at 350°. Cool on wire rack. (Frost if desired. Cream cheese, lemon juice, and powdered sugar mixture goes well with this.) Makes 6 generous servings.

Sarajane's Zucchini Bundt Cake

Flour   2 cups
Rice flour   1 cup (or potato flour)
Salt   ½ teaspoon
Soda   1 teaspoon
Baking powder   1 teaspoon
Sugar   2 cups
Eggs   3
Cooking oil   1 cup
Vanilla   2 teaspoons
Chopped nuts   1 cup
Crushed pineapple   1 cup drained
Zucchini   2 cups grated and drained

Mix all ingredients together and bake in greased bundt pan at 325° until it tests done. Good served with cream cheese. Serves 8.

Granola Zucchini Cake

Brown sugar 1 cup
Sugar 1 cup
Eggs 4
Cooking oil 1 cup
Flour 2 cups
Soda 1 teaspoon
Baking powder 2 teaspoons
Salt ½ teaspoon
Nutmeg and cinnamon 1 teaspoon each
Vanilla and coconut extract 1 teaspoon each
Granola 1 cup, any style
Chopped nuts ½ cup
Zucchini 4 cups shredded and squeezed dry

Beat sugar, eggs, and oil together. Stir next 4 ingredients together; add along with seasonings and stir well. Stir in granola, nuts, and zucchini. Pour into greased and floured 9 × 13-inch pan. Bake about 45 to 55 minutes at 350°, or until it tests done. Cool on wire rack. Good served warm, with whipped cream. Can be frozen; cool and cut into squares before freezing. Serves 10 to 12.

Zucchini Crumb Cake

Margarine ¼ cup, softened
Sugar 1 cup
Egg 1
Flour 2 cups
Baking powder 1 tablespoon
Salt ¼ teaspoon
Milk 1 cup
Zucchini 1 cup finely chopped (not shredded)
Flour 1 cup
Sugar 1 cup
Cinnamon 2 teaspoons
Margarine ½ cup

Beat ¼ cup softened margarine, 1 cup sugar, and egg together. Stir 2 cups flour, baking powder, and salt together; add alternately with milk. Beat until batter is creamy. Stir in chopped zucchini. Pour into well-buttered 8- or 9-inch round cake pan. To make crumbs, blend remaining ingredients with pastry blender until crumbs form. Sprinkle batter with crumb mixture. Bake about 25 to 30 minutes at 350°, until it tests done. Serve as coffee cake, or for dessert cake with ice cream. Serves 6 to 8.

Easy Zucchini Pineapple Jellyroll Cake

Crushed pineapple   1 cup drained
Zucchini   1¼ cups finely diced (can be firm flesh of a very large one, peeled)
Brown sugar   ½ cup firmly packed
Sugar   ½ cup
Eggs   3, separated
Pineapple juice   2 tablespoons
Pineapple extract   ¼ teaspoon
Flour   1 cup
Salt   ¼ teaspoon
Baking powder   1 teaspoon
Powdered sugar
Whipped cream

Drain pineapple well and save the juice. Sprinkle pineapple in greased 9 × 13 × 2-inch pan. (Smaller pan makes the roll too thick.) Scatter zucchini over pineapple. Sprinkle with brown sugar and pat it down with your hand.

Mix sugar and egg yolks. Stir in pineapple juice and extract, then flour, salt, and baking powder. Beat egg whites until stiff, fold into batter. Spoon batter over zucchini mixture in pan, smooth the top. Bake at 375° for 15 to 18 minutes, or until cake tests done. Do not overbake.

Loosen cake from sides of pan. Turn it out, upside down, on clean dish towel sprinkled with powdered sugar. Trim off any crisp edges of cake. While still hot, roll the cake, starting at the 9-inch end (pick up edge of cloth to start it rolling). Wrap it in the cloth until it is cool. Slice and top with whipped cream for an elegant dessert. Best eaten the day you bake it.

Molasses Cake

Egg 1, beaten
Sugar ⅓ cup
Molasses ½ cup
Shortening ¼ cup, melted
Nuts ½ cup chopped
Flour 2 cups
Salt 1 teaspoon
Soda 1 teaspoon
Baking powder ¾ teaspoon
Dry lemon peel 1½ teaspoons grated
Sour milk ⅔ cup*
Zucchini 2 cups finely diced, not grated (can be firm flesh of very
  large one)

Mix egg, sugar, molasses, and shortening; add nuts. Mix together flour, salt, soda, baking powder, and lemon peel; add alternately with sour milk. Stir in chopped zucchini. Bake in greased and floured 9 × 13-inch pan at 350° for 35 to 40 minutes. This is a moist cake, good with whipped cream or sweetened cream cheese frosting.
* To make sour milk, add 1 teaspoon lemon juice to ½ cup whole or skim milk. Let stand 5 minutes before using.

Chocolate Zucchini Cake

Margarine   ½ cup, softened
Vegetable oil   ½ cup
Sugar   1¾ cups
Eggs   2
Vanilla   1 teaspoon
Sour milk   ½ cup*
Flour   2½ cups
Cocoa   4 tablespoons
Baking powder   ½ teaspoon
Soda   1 teaspoon
Cinnamon   ½ teaspoon
Cloves   ½ teaspoon
Zucchini   2 cups finely diced, not shredded (works best with firm flesh of
     very large one)
Chocolate chips   ¼ cup

Cream margarine, oil, and sugar. Add eggs, vanilla, and sour milk; beat with mixer. Mix together all the dry ingredients and add to creamed mixture; beat well with mixer. Stir in diced zucchini. Spoon batter into greased and floured 9 × 12 × 2-inch pan; sprinkle top with chocolate chips. Bake at 325° for 40 to 45 minutes or until toothpick or cake tester comes out clean and dry. This really needs no frosting; it is moist and very tender.

Tip: To finely dice large zucchini, slice it crosswise in ¼-inch slices. Take each slice, chop it in half, and remove and discard center half-moon of pulp and seeds. The remaining half circle of firm flesh, ¼-inch thick, can be easily diced into ¼-inch cubes. If skin is tender it will not need to be peeled.

* To make sour milk, add 1 teaspoon lemon juice to ½ cup whole or skim milk. Let stand 5 minutes before using.

Fruitcake

Zucchini 1 cup diced, not shredded
Brandy flavoring   1 teaspoon
Sugar 1 cup
Apple juice 1 cup
Margarine ⅓ cup
Water 2 tablespoons
Dates ½ cup chopped
Brandy flavoring 1 teaspoon
Flour 2 cups
Salt 1 teaspoon
Baking powder 1 teaspoon
Soda 1 teaspoon
Mixed candied fruits ½ cup
Nuts ½ cup chopped

Sprinkle diced zucchini with brandy flavoring; set aside. Combine sugar, apple juice, margarine, water, and dates; bring to boil. Boil 2 minutes; cool. Add brandy flavoring. Mix together flour, salt, baking powder, and soda; stir into apple juice mixture. Add zucchini, candied fruits, and nuts; mix well. Spoon into 2 greased and paper-lined 9 × 5 × 3-inch loaf pans. Bake at 325° for 1 hour or until it tests done. Cool and chill before cutting.

Zucchinisauce Cake

Yellow or green zucchini   3 cups cubed (can be firm flesh of large one)
Frozen apple juice   1 cup undiluted
Margarine   ½ cup, softened
Sugar   1½ cups
Egg   1
Flour   2½ cups
Soda   1½ teaspoons
Salt   1 teaspoon
Cloves   ½ teaspoon
Allspice   ½ teaspoon
Cinnamon   ¼ teaspoon
Walnuts   ½ cup chopped

Simmer zucchini in ½ cup frozen apple juice until tender (thaw remaining ½ cup juice). Whirl in blender; set aside. Cream margarine, sugar, and egg until fluffy. Add blended zucchini sauce; mix well. Mix together flour, soda, salt, and spices; add alternately with remaining ½ cup thawed apple juice. Beat well. Stir in nuts. Bake in greased and floured 9 × 13 × 2-inch pan, at 350° approximately 40 minutes. Frost as desired.

Honey Cake

Margarine   ½ cup, softened
Vanilla   1 teaspoon
Eggs   2
Honey   ⅔ cup
Water   ½ cup
Flour   1¾ cups
Soda   1 teaspoon
Baking powder   ½ teaspoon
Salt   ½ teaspoon
Zucchini   1 cup finely diced
Nuts   ½ cup chopped (or ½ cup ground sunflower seeds)

Combine margarine, vanilla, eggs, and honey; beat with mixer. Beat in water. Add dry ingredients; mix well. Stir in zucchini and nuts. Bake at 350° in greased and floured 9 × 13 × 2-inch pan for 25 to 30 minutes, or until cake tests done. Good with sweetened cream cheese or topped with fruit.

Sourdough Zucchini Cake

Shortening ½ cup
Sugar 2 cups
Eggs 2
Sourdough starter 1½ cups
Zucchini 1½ cups grated
Cinnamon 2½ teaspoons
Cloves 1 teaspoon
Allspice 1 teaspoon
Salt 1½ teaspoons
Soda 1½ teaspoons
Sugar 2 tablespoons
Flour 2 cups
White raisins ½ cup
Walnuts ½ cup chopped
Lemon Glaze Icing

Cream shortening and sugar; beat in eggs. Stir in sourdough starter, zucchini, and spices. Mix salt, soda, and sugar; sprinkle over batter, and stir in. Add flour and stir until smooth; add raisins and walnuts, stir well. Pour into greased and floured 9 × 13 × 2-inch pan. Bake at 350° for 35 to 40 minutes, or until it tests done. Frost with very thin Lemon Glaze Icing.

Lemon Glaze Icing

Margarine 2 tablespoons
Powdered sugar 2 cups sifted
Water 1 tablespoon, boiling
Lemon juice 2 tablespoons

Melt margarine; beat in sugar, boiling water, and lemon juice.

Upside-Down Gingerbread

Margarine   ¼ cup
Brown sugar   ¾ cup firmly packed
Zucchini   1½ cups diced (can be firm flesh of very large one, peeled and
    center pulp removed)
Unsweetened coconut   1 cup shredded or grated
Vegetable oil   ⅓ cup
Egg   1
Molasses   ½ cup
Honey   ½ cup
Sour milk or buttermilk   1 cup
Flour   2½ cups
Ginger   2 teaspoons
Cinnamon   ½ teaspoon
Soda   1¾ teaspoons
Salt   ½ teaspoon
Zucchini   ½ cup finely diced

Grease sides of 9 × 13 × 2-inch pan (or two 8 × 8-inch pans). Melt
margarine in bottom of pan or divide for 2 pans. Spread brown sugar over.
Mix 1½ cups zucchini and coconut together, layer over brown sugar, and pat
down gently with your hands.

Mix together oil, egg, molasses, and honey; beat. Add sour milk and beat.
Add remaining dry ingredients; beat well. Stir in ½ cup zucchini. Pour batter
over zucchini–coconut layer and spread carefully. Bake at 350° for approximately 25 to 35 minutes or until it tests done. Turn it out on platter while hot.
This is a moist cake with frostinglike topping.

White Cake

Vegetable oil ¼ cup
Margarine ¼ cup, softened
Sugar 1 cup
Flour 2 cups
Cornstarch 2 tablespoons
Baking powder 3 teaspoons
Milk ⅔ cup (can be skim milk)
Almond extract ½ teaspoon
Lemon peel ½ teaspoon grated
Zucchini 1 cup finely chopped, not grated
Egg whites 3

Cream oil and margarine; add sugar and beat until fluffy. Mix together flour, cornstarch, and baking powder. Add alternately* with milk to the creamed mixture; beat until smooth. Add almond extract and lemon peel. Stir in zucchini. Beat egg whites stiff; fold into batter. Bake in 2 greased and floured 9-inch layer pans or sheet pan, at 375° for 25 to 30 minutes.
* Cake will be lighter in texture if dry ingredients are sifted into creamed mixture.

Zucchini Wedding Cake Decoration

Make double recipe of your favorite boiled or powdered sugar icing. Divide into three bowls—⅔ of icing in 1 bowl, the rest divided into 2 smaller bowls. With vegetable coloring, tint large bowl of icing a pale green, tint other 2 bowls of icing medium green and dark green. Spread tops and sides of all cake layers with pale green; decorate with other 2 shades of green by hand or with pastry tube.

Candy (using method from Zucchini Pie recipe) thin slices of small zucchini; twist each slice a little and stick into frosting around top edges of each layer. Place zucchini slices flat against frosted sides of layers and frosting rosettes against centers of slices.

Put layers together, tier style, with small zucchini (cut the same length) used as supporting pillars. Rest upper layers on rounds of white cardboard, cut to size of layers, and zucchini pillars will not poke up into layer above. Rest bottom of each zucchini pillar on a toothpick laid horizontally to keep it from sinking into layer below; frosting covers toothpick. To anchor, insert 1 toothpick vertically halfway up into bottom of each pillar and other half into layer beneath.

Iced Sweeties

Sugar   ⅔ cup
Margarine   2 tablespoons
Egg   1
Flour   1½ cups
Baking powder   1 teaspoon
Salt   ⅛ teaspoon
Milk   ⅔ cup
Zucchini   ¾ cup diced, not shredded
Icing

Beat sugar, margarine, and egg together. Mix dry ingredients together; add alternately with milk. Stir in zucchini; mix well. Spread very thin on a greased and floured cookie sheet. Bake at 350° until lightly browned and cake tests done. Pour icing (below) over cake while hot; bake at 400° until top begins to bubble. Remove and cool; cut into squares.

Baked-On Icing

Brown sugar   9 tablespoons firmly packed
Cream or milk   2 tablespoons
Margarine   4 tablespoons
Salt   pinch
Vanilla   1 teaspoon
Coconut and/or nuts   ½ cup chopped (or mixture of both)

Cook sugar, milk, and margarine over low heat until thick. Add salt, vanilla, coconut, and/or nuts. Pour over cake as instructed above.

Coffee Bars

Flour   ½ cup
Baking powder   1 teaspoon
Salt   ½ teaspoon
Sugar   ¾ cup
Egg   1
Instant coffee   1 tablespoon, dissolved in
Water   1 teaspoon, hot
Zucchini   1 cup peeled and diced (can be from large one)
Nuts   ½ cup chopped

Mix together flour, baking powder, salt, and sugar. Add egg, coffee, and zucchini; mix well. Stir in chopped nuts. Spread in greased and floured 8 × 8-inch pan; bake at 350° for 25 minutes. Cut into bars when cool.

Cinnamon Zucchini Brownies

Margarine   ⅓ cup, softened
Brown sugar   1 cup firmly packed
Egg   1
Vanilla   1½ teaspoons
Flour   1 cup
Cinnamon   1½ teaspoons
Baking powder   ¼ teaspoon
Salt   ½ teaspoon
Nutmeg   ¼ teaspoon
Zucchini   1 cup chopped, not shredded (can be firm flesh of very
    large one)
Nuts   ½ cup chopped

Mix margarine and brown sugar; beat until fluffy. Add egg and vanilla; beat well. Add mixed dry ingredients and stir. Add zucchini and nuts; mix. Bake in greased and floured 9 × 9-inch pan at 350° for 25 to 30 minutes. Cool in pan; cut into bars.

Blond Brownies

Margarine   ⅓ cup
Water   1 tablespoon, hot
Brown sugar   1 cup firmly packed
Egg   1
Vanilla   1 teaspoon
Flour   1 cup
Baking powder   1 teaspoon
Soda   ⅛ teaspoon
Salt   ½ teaspoon
Zucchini   ¾ cup peeled and diced, not shredded (can be firm flesh of
   very large one)
Nuts   ½ cup chopped
Butterscotch chips   ¼ cup

In large pan melt margarine with hot water; add brown sugar and beat well.
Cool. Add egg and vanilla; beat. Mix dry ingredients together and add to
sugar mixture. Stir in zucchini and nuts. Pour mixture into greased and
floured 9 × 9-inch pan; sprinkle with butterscotch chips. Bake at 350° for 20
to 25 minutes. Cool in pan; cut into bars.

Zucchalmond Squares

Zucchini   1½ cups peeled and finely chopped
Almond extract   1 teaspoon
Egg whites   2
Sugar   ⅓ cup
Flour   ½ cup
Baking powder   1 teaspoon
Salt   ¼ teaspoon
Nuts   ½ cup chopped

Sprinkle chopped zucchini with almond extract; set aside. Beat egg whites
until foamy; add sugar and beat thoroughly with electric mixer. Mix together
dry ingredients and add; fold in nuts and zucchini. Spoon into greased 8 ×
8-inch pan. Bake at 350° for 40 minutes. Cool in pan; cut into squares.

Orange Zucchini Squares

Sugar 1 cup
Flour 1½ cups
Soda 1 teaspoon
Salt ½ teaspoon
Cinnamon 1 teaspoon
Baking powder 1 teaspoon
Nuts ½ cup chopped
Zucchini 1 cup grated, drained
Egg whites 2, lightly beaten
Frozen orange juice ½ cup thawed
Vegetable oil 4 tablespoons
Orange peel 1½ teaspoons grated

Mix dry ingredients together; stir in nuts and zucchini. To beaten egg whites add the orange juice and oil. Fold into dry ingredients and add orange peel. Spoon into greased and floured 9 × 13 × 2-inch pan. Bake at 350° for 40 to 45 minutes or until toothpick inserted in center comes out dry and clean. Cool; cut into squares. Can be drizzled with thin orange icing if desired.

Frosted Zucchini Spice Drops

Margarine   ½ cup, softened
Brown sugar   1½ cups
Egg   1
Flour   2½ cups
Soda   ¼ teaspoon
Baking powder   1 teaspoon
Salt   ½ teaspoon
Nutmeg   ½ teaspoon
Cinnamon   1 teaspoon
Cloves   ½ teaspoon
Milk   ¼ cup
Zucchini   1 cup finely chopped or diced
Walnuts   ½ cup chopped
Confectioner's Icing

Cream margarine and brown sugar together. Beat in egg. Stir dry ingredients together, then add to creamed mixture. Stir in milk, then zucchini and walnuts. Drop by spoonfuls on lightly oiled baking sheet; bake at 400° for 10 to 12 minutes or until lightly browned. Frost while warm. Makes 4 to 5 dozen.

Confectioner's Icing

Butter or margarine   1 tablespoon, softened
Milk   2 tablespoons
Powdered sugar   2½ cups
Vanilla   1 teaspoon
Salt   ⅛ teaspoon

Mix frosting ingredients; spread on warm cookies.

Frosted Cookie Favorite

Margarine   ½ cup, softened
Brown sugar   1 cup firmly packed
Sugar   ½ cup
Eggs   2
Canned milk   1 cup undiluted
Vanilla   1 teaspoon
Flour   2⅔ cups
Soda   ½ teaspoon
Walnuts   1 cup chopped
Zucchini   1 cup diced, not shredded
Butter Glaze Frosting

Mix margarine and sugars; beat. Add eggs; mix well. Stir in canned milk and vanilla. Mix flour and soda together; stir in. Add nuts. Chill 1 hour. Stir in zucchini, mixing well. Drop from tablespoon 2 inches apart on greased cookie sheet. Bake at 375° for 8 to 10 minutes, until delicately brown. Do not overbake. While warm, frost and garnish with pieces of nut.

Butter Glaze Frosting

Melt 2 tablespoons margarine; beat in 2 cups sifted powdered sugar and ¼ cup undiluted canned milk.

Lemon Cookies

Margarine ½ cup
Sugar ½ cup
Honey ½ cup
Egg 1
Lemon rind 2 teaspoons grated
Flour 2 cups
Salt ½ teaspoon
Baking powder 1 teaspoon
Zucchini 1 cup chopped, not shredded
Wheat germ 1 cup

Beat margarine, sugar, and honey together until fluffy. Add egg and lemon rind; beat well. Mix together flour, salt, and baking powder; stir into sugar mixture. Add zucchini and ½ cup of the wheat germ. Refrigerate one hour or longer. If dough is not quite stiff enough to roll into balls, add more wheat germ (some zucchini have more moisture than others and would need this). Shape dough into 1-inch balls; roll balls in remaining ½ cup wheat germ. Place on ungreased cookie sheet; flatten slightly. Place on oven rack above center of oven; bake at 400° for 8 minutes or until edges of cookies are just lightly browned. Remove to wire racks to cool. Store in covered cookie jar. Makes 5 dozen.

Country Cookies

Margarine ½ cup, softened
Sugar 1 cup
Egg 1
Flour 1½ cups
Salt ½ teaspoon
Soda ½ teaspoon
Cinnamon 1 teaspoon
Allspice ½ teaspoon
Potato flakes 1¾ cups dry crushed
Nuts ½ cup chopped
Zucchini 1 cup diced, not shredded
Milk ¼ cup

Beat margarine, sugar, and egg together until fluffy. Mix together flour, salt, soda, and spices. Stir potato flakes, nuts, and zucchini into flour mixture; add to sugar mixture alternately with milk. Mix well after each addition. Drop from teaspoon on greased cookie sheet. Bake at 350° for 12 to 14 minutes. Cool on brown paper. Makes about 4 dozen.

Pineapple Cookies

Vegetable oil ½ cup
Margarine ½ cup, softened
Brown sugar 2 cups firmly packed
Eggs 2
Frozen pineapple juice 2 tablespoons
Pineapple extract ½ teaspoon
Vanilla ¼ teaspoon
Zucchini 1 cup grated (can be firm flesh of very large one)
Flour 3 cups
Wheat germ 1 cup
Soda ½ teaspoon
Baking powder 1 teaspoon
Salt ½ teaspoon
Quick-cooking noninstant oatmeal ¾ cup uncooked

Cream oil, margarine, and sugar. Add eggs; mix well by hand or with mixer. Add pineapple juice and flavorings; beat. Stir in grated zucchini. Mix dry ingredients except oatmeal together; add to creamed mixture; stir until all are moistened. Add oatmeal; mix. Chill dough for 20 minutes; drop from teaspoon onto greased cookie sheet. Bake at 350° for 10 minutes. Remove from cookie sheet at once; cool on brown paper.

Zucchini Date Pudding

Eggs 2
Sugar ⅓ cup
Flour 2 tablespoons
Baking powder 1 teaspoon
Chopped nuts 1 cup (walnuts or pecans)
Dates 1 cup chopped
Zucchini 1 cup chopped, not shredded
Cinnamon ½ teaspoon
Sugar 1 teaspoon

Beat eggs and ⅓ cup sugar together until thickened. Mix flour and baking powder, stir into nuts and dates, and mix this into sugar–egg ingredients. Fold in chopped zucchini. Put into shallow buttered 7 × 11-inch casserole. Mix cinnamon and 1 teaspoon sugar and sprinkle over top. Bake about 30 minutes at 300°, or until set. Serve warm with cream or whipped cream. Serves 6 to 8.

Golden Zucchini Custard

Golden zucchini 1 pound, cubed
Milk 1 cup
Dry powdered skim milk ⅓ cup
Eggs 3
Egg yolks 1
Sugar ½ cup
Vanilla 1 teaspoon
Salt ⅛ teaspoon
Nutmeg to sprinkle on tops

Steam zucchini until tender, put in blender container with milk, blend to puree, add dry powdered milk, and blend. In large bowl, beat eggs and yolks lightly with sugar, vanilla, and salt. Stir in zucchini puree. Pour into buttered Pyrex custard cups, sprinkle with nutmeg, and place in 9 × 13-inch baking pan. Pour boiling water around custard cups, to come halfway up sides of cups. Bake at 300° for 45 to 55 minutes, until a knife inserted in center comes out clean. Serve warm or chilled. Refrigerate any custards not eaten the same day as baked. Serves 6 to 10, depending upon size of custard cups.

Zucchini Bread Pudding with Meringue

Hot milk 1 cup
Butter 2 tablespoons
Eggs 2, beaten
Egg yolks 2, beaten
Cinnamon ½ teaspoon
Nutmeg or mace ¼ teaspoon
Vanilla 1½ teaspoons
Sugar ½ cup
Bread 1 cup cubed
Bread or cake crumbs ½ cup
Zucchini ¾ cup shredded (drained) or chopped
Raisins or chopped dates ½ cup
Flaked coconut ½ cup
Egg whites 2
Sugar 2 tablespoons
Vanilla 3 drops

Heat milk and butter together; pour slowly onto beaten eggs and egg yolks. Add cinnamon, nutmeg, 1½ teaspoons vanilla, and ½ cup sugar. In separate bowl, mix bread, bread crumbs, zucchini, raisins, and coconut and place in a buttered 8 × 8-inch casserole. Pour milk–egg mixture over bread and zucchini. Bake at 325° for 30 minutes or until set. Beat egg whites, gradually adding 2 tablespoons sugar. Continue beating, adding 3 drops vanilla, until stiff peaks form. Mound on top of baked pudding and bake at 350° until meringue is delicately browned. Serves 6 to 8.

Upside-Down Pudding

Flour   1 tablespoon
Powdered orange peel   1 teaspoon
Cinnamon   1 teaspoon
Zucchini   3 cups peeled and cut in ¼-inch cubes
Honey   ½ cup
Lemon juice   ½ teaspoon
Flour   1 cup unsifted
Baking powder   2 teaspoons
Salt   ½ teaspoon
Margarine   ¼ cup, softened
Egg   1
Milk   3 tablespoons
Honey   2 tablespoons

Mix 1 tablespoon flour, orange peel, and cinnamon with diced zucchini; stir in ½ cup honey and lemon juice. Spoon into oiled 8 × 8-inch pan. Mix 1 cup flour, baking powder, and salt. Cut in margarine. Combine egg, milk, and 2 tablespoons honey; add to dry ingredients and stir until all are just moistened. Using 2 knives, spread on zucchini mixture and bake at 350° for 25 minutes. Serve slightly warm with cream or whipped cream.

This one is a real puzzler unless you know the secret—is it apple? Is it pear? No one will guess unless you tell.

Steamed Pudding

Margarine   1 tablespoon, softened
Brown sugar   ½ cup firmly packed
Egg   1, beaten
Orange extract   ½ teaspoon
Ground cardamom   ½ teaspoon
Flour   1¾ cups
Baking powder   2 teaspoons
Salt   ¼ teaspoon
Milk   ½ cup
Zucchini   1 cup diced in ¼-inch cubes
Orange Sauce

Cream margarine and sugar; add egg and orange extract; beat well. Mix together dry ingredients; add to creamed mixture alternately with milk. Stir in zucchini. Spoon into oiled custard cups or individual steam-pudding molds. Cover; steam 1 hour for large pudding, or 45 minutes for small ones. Serve with orange sauce. Serves 4 to 6.

Orange Sauce

Frozen orange juice   1 cup undiluted, thawed
Cornstarch   1½ tablespoons
Lemon juice   ½ teaspoon
Butter or margarine   1 tablespoon
Salt   pinch

Combine and bring to boil; simmer until thick and clear, stirring often.

Honey Pudding

Green or golden zucchini 2 pounds medium (or firm flesh of a very
    large one)
Honey ¼ cup
Salt ⅛ teaspoon
Pumpkin pie spice ½ teaspoon
Cinnamon 1 teaspoon
Milk ⅓ cup
Egg 1
Flour ⅓ cup
Nutmeg
Shredded coconut

Trim ends from zucchini; steam until tender. Put into blender container with
honey, salt, spices, and milk. Blend until smooth. Add egg and blend. Stir in
flour; mix well. Turn into custard cups; sprinkle tops with nutmeg and
shredded coconut. Bake at 300° for 1 hour. Serve slightly warm or cold with
sweetened whipped cream. Serves 4.

Zucchini Meringue Pie

Egg yolks 3
Sugar 5 tablespoons
Cornstarch 1 teaspoon
Lemon rind ⅓ teaspoon grated
Vanilla ½ teaspoon
Milk 1 cup, boiling
Pastry
Zucchini Filling
Egg whites 4
Salt pinch
Vanilla 1 teaspoon
Sugar 6 tablespoons
Green candied fruit or green crystallized sugar garnish

Mix egg yolks, 5 tablespoons sugar, cornstarch, and lemon rind. Add ½ teaspoon vanilla and boiling milk. Simmer to thicken. Put aside to cool. Prepare
Pastry and Zucchini Filling. Spread cooled custard in precooked pie shells.
Top with well-drained Zucchini Filling. Whip egg whites with salt until very
stiff. Add remaining vanilla and sugar; mix well. Cover custard mixture with
meringue and bake at 300° for 15 to 20 minutes until meringue is nicely
browned. Garnish with candied fruit. Makes 2 pies or 6 tarts.

Pastry

Sugar 2 tablespoons
Unsalted butter 1 cup
Salt pinch
Flour 2 cups
Water 5 to 6 tablespoons, cold

Mix sugar, butter, salt, and flour until homogenous. Add cold water gradually, enough to bind. Do not overwork dough while adding water or it may become rubbery. Roll out pastry; line 2 pie tins or 6 tart pans. Prebake shells at 450° until firm, but not browned.

Zucchini Filling

Sugar 2 pounds
Lemon 1, sliced
Vanilla 1 tablespoon
Water 2 cups
Zucchini 2½ pounds small

Combine sugar, lemon, vanilla, and water; bring to boil. Wash zucchini; trim off and discard ends. Slice into ½-inch rounds; put into boiling syrup. Cook until transparent and slightly candied. Drain. Reserve syrup for other usages.

Impossible Zucchini Coconut Pie

Eggs 4
Sugar ¾ cup
Flaked or shredded coconut 1 cup
Milk 2 cups
Vanilla 1½ teaspoons
Salt a pinch
Margarine ¼ cup, melted
Buttermilk baking mix (biscuit mix) ½ cup
Zucchini ¾ cup finely diced

Place all ingredients except zucchini in a blender container. Cover and blend on high speed for 15 seconds. Stir in zucchini. Pour into a greased 10-inch pie plate. Bake at 350° for 45 to 55 minutes or until a knife inserted in center comes out clean. Cool. Bake several hours before serving for best flavor. Serves 6.

Rhubarb Zucchini Pie

Zucchini   3 cups diced
Rhubarb   1 cup sliced
Sugar   1¼ cups
Apple pie spices   1½ teaspoons
Salt   pinch
Flour   ¼ cup
Frozen concentrated apple juice   ¼ cup thawed
Eggs   2, beaten
Pastry   for 2-crust 9-inch pie
Sugar   to sprinkle on crust

Combine all ingredients except pastry. Pour into unbaked pastry shell, cover with top crust and cut slits for steam to escape. Sprinkle lightly with sugar. Bake at 400° for 20 minutes, then at 350° until golden brown and done.

Vanilla Ice Cream*

Plain gelatin   1½ teaspoons
Cold water   ¼ cup
Zucchini   1½ cups peeled and diced
Honey   ½ cup
Vanilla   1 teaspoon
Evaporated canned milk   1 13-ounce can
Milk or cream

Soften gelatin in water. Simmer zucchini in honey until tender. Blend well in blender. Add softened gelatin, vanilla, and canned milk. Stir well. Add enough milk to bring mixture up to 22 or 23 ounces. Chill mixture for 3 hours. Pour into ice cream machine and freeze until done. Makes 1 quart.
* Recipes for use in Salton Ice Cream Machine.
Variations:
   Date Coconut Ice Cream. Make only 21 ounces of Vanilla Ice Cream
      mixture, then add ½ cup dates and ¼ cup shredded coconut after
      ½ hour of freezing process.
   Butter Pecan Ice Cream. Make only 21 ounces of Vanilla Ice Cream mix-
      ture. Saute ½ cup chopped pecans in 1 tablespoon butter; cool.
      Add this to mixture after ½ hour of freezing process.

Butterscotch Milk Shake

Zucchini ½ cup sliced
Honey 2 tablespoons
Butterscotch flavoring 2 teaspoons
Cold water 2 tablespoons
Dry powdered skim milk ¾ cup
Ice cubes crushed

Put all ingredients in blender, except ice cubes. Zoom until well blended. Add crushed ice cubes, one at a time, with blender on high, until shake is thick. This may take 5 to 7 cubes, depending on ice cube size. Work quickly for a really thick shake. Serve at once. Serves 2.
Variation: Substitute 2 teaspoons chocolate flavoring extract for butterscotch flavoring.
Note: Peel zucchini if peeling is tough or if you want to be sneaky!

Pineapple Milk Shake

Frozen concentrated pineapple juice ½ 6-ounce can
Zucchini ½ cup sliced
Dry powdered milk ¾ cup
Ice cubes crushed

Directions same as for Butterscotch Milk Shake. Serves 2.

Meatless Entrees

Cheese Steaks with Zucchini and Sour Cream

Low-fat small curd cottage cheese 2 cups
Butter 2 tablespoons, melted
Eggs 2, beaten
White pepper ½ teaspoon
Flour ¾ cup
Oil for frying ½ cup
Zucchini 3 cups coarsely chopped
Dairy sour cream 1 cup
Vinegar 1 tablespoon
Fresh dill 2 tablespoons chopped (or 1 tablespoon dried dill weed)
Sugar ¼ teaspoon
Onion powder ¼ teaspoon
Salt ½ teaspoon
Fresh ground pepper ½ teaspoon

Mash cottage cheese and mix with butter and eggs. Stir in pepper and flour. Add more flour if necessary to make a stiff dough. Spoon out ½ cup at a time, form into patties on floured surface. Fry patties in hot oil until golden, turn and fry other side. Keep patties in warm oven while preparing zucchini and sour cream sauce.

Steam zucchini until barely tender (or cook in small amount of water and drain well). Combine with remaining ingredients; heat slowly until very hot, but do not boil. To serve, spoon out small serving of zucchini mixture, place cheese patty on it, spoon on topping of more zucchini mixture. Serves 4 to 6.

Potato Bake

Zucchini 3 cups sliced
Vegetable oil 1 tablespoon
Tomatoes 4, quartered (or 1 16-ounce can tomatoes, drained)
Flour 1 tablespoon
Onion salt 1 teaspoon
Frozen french-fried potatoes 1 10-ounce package, thawed
Medium cheddar cheese 4 thick slices

Saute zucchini in oil for 5 minutes. Add tomatoes; saute until well heated through. Sprinkle with flour and onion salt; spoon into shallow oiled casserole. Cover with thawed potatoes and bake at 350° for 20 minutes. Top with cheddar cheese slices and bake an additional 10 minutes. Serves 4.

Cottage Cheese Casserole

Zucchini   2 cups sliced
Onion   1 cup chopped
Cottage cheese   2 cups
Eggs   3, beaten
Cooked rice   1 cup
Salt and pepper   to taste
Soft bread crumbs   ½ cup
Parmesan cheese   ½ cup grated
Butter   ¼ cup, melted

Saute zucchini and onion; remove from heat and set aside. Mix cottage cheese, eggs, rice, and seasonings. Put half of zucchini and onion in oiled casserole, top with half of the cheese mixture, and repeat layers. Mix bread crumbs and parmesan, sprinkle over casserole, then drizzle with melted butter. Bake about 40 minutes at 350°. Serves 6.

Colorful Casserole

Carrots   3 cups sliced and chopped
Vegetable bouillon   1 cube
Water   ½ cup
Zucchini   3 cups sliced and diced (can be from very large one)
Seasoned salt   1 teaspoon
Thyme   ¼ teaspoon
Parsley   1 tablespoon chopped
Fresh ground pepper
Eggs   2
Milk   1½ cups
Bread crumbs or cracker crumbs   1½ cups
Medium cheddar cheese   1 cup shredded

Chop carrots with food chopper or whirl in blender to chop coarsely. Dissolve bouillon in boiling water; add carrots; cover and simmer slowly 10 minutes. Add diced zucchini; simmer a few minutes, stirring occasionally. Drain; add seasonings. Beat eggs with milk; add crumbs and cheddar cheese; stir in vegetables. Turn into greased casserole; bake at 350° for 40 minutes or until set. Serves 6 to 8.

Baked Vegetable Rice

Water 1½ cups, boiling
Chicken bouillon 1 cube
Salt ½ teaspoon
Brown rice ½ cup
Carrots ½ cup, shredded
Onion ½ large, chopped
Celery 1 stalk, thinly sliced
Zucchini 2 cups thinly sliced
Parsley ¼ cup chopped
Leftover vegetables any cooked ones
Eggs 2
Milk ½ cup
Medium cheddar cheese ½ cup grated

Combine first 7 ingredients in shallow casserole; bake at 350° for 15 minutes. Add zucchini, parsley, and leftover vegetables. Bake 15 minutes longer or until rice has absorbed all liquid. Stir eggs and milk together and stir into hot rice mixture. Top with cheese. Bake another 30 minutes or until set and browned. Serves 6.

Continental Vegetables

Zucchini 2 cups sliced
Green pepper 1, diced
Carrots 1 cup shredded
Shallots ¼ cup sliced (or use 1 chopped green onion plus 1 small clove garlic)
Vegetable oil 2 tablespoons
Salt and pepper to taste
Yogurt or dairy sour cream ¾ cup
Parmesan cheese ½ cup grated
Parsley 2 tablespoons chopped
Thyme ½ teaspoon crumbled
Crumbs 2 tablespoons, buttered
Parmesan cheese 2 tablespoons

In large skillet, saute vegetables in oil for 5 minutes. Season to taste with salt and pepper. Mix yogurt or sour cream with cheese, parsley, and thyme. Stir into vegetables; spoon into buttered casserole. Sprinkle top with mixed crumbs and parmesan cheese. Bake at 350° for 30 minutes. Serves 4.

Zucchini-Filled Potato Roll

Potatoes   6 large, peeled, cooked tender
Butter   3 tablespoons
Salt   1 teaspoon
White pepper   ½ teaspoon
Eggs   2, beaten
Flour   ¼ cup
Carrots   1 cup diced, cooked
Mushrooms   1 4-ounce can stems and pieces
Zucchini   1 cup chopped, steamed 5 minutes
Butter   1 tablespoon
Butter   2 tablespoons, softened
Parmesan cheese   ½ cup grated

Mash or rice cooked potatoes; mix in 3 tablespoons butter, salt, and pepper, then eggs and flour. On lightly floured waxed paper, pat potatoes out into long flat rectangle, about ¾ to 1 inch thick, six inches wide. Saute cooked carrots, mushrooms, and chopped zucchini in 1 tablespoon butter. Spread vegetables along center of potato surface. Form potato into roll around vegetables. Brush roll with remaining butter; sprinkle it with parmesan cheese. Bake it about 15 minutes at 450° on greased cookie sheet. Let it stand 5 minutes, then cut into slices. Serve hot. Serves 6 generously.

Zucchini Ring

Zucchini   5 cups cubed (can be peeled cubes of very large one)
Skim milk powder   3 tablespoons
Wheat germ   4 tablespoons
Vegetable oil or melted margarine   2 tablespoons
Eggs   2, beaten
Onion salt
Fresh ground pepper

Peel and cube zucchini; steam until very tender. Drain and mash in colander, reserving the juice. Measure ¼ cup of this juice; add skim milk powder, wheat germ, oil, and beaten eggs. Beat in mashed zucchini. Season with onion salt and pepper. Bake in small oiled tube pan at 300° for 45 minutes. Remove from pan to hot platter. Center can be filled with vegetable of contrasting color, or creamed meat or fish. Serves 4.

Vegetarian Rice-Stuffed Zucchini

Zucchini 3 6-inch size, or 1 12-inch size
Mushrooms 2 cups sliced (or 3 4-ounce cans of stems and pieces)
Onions ¾ cup chopped
Cooking oil 2 tablespoons
Jack cheese 2 cups shredded
Eggs 3, beaten
Brown rice 1 cup cooked until barely tender
Roasted sunflower seeds ¾ cup
Fenugreek ½ teaspoon (or 1 teaspoon curry powder)
Seasoning salt ½ teaspoon
Fresh ground pepper ½ teaspoon
Fresh parsley 1 tablespoon chopped

Steam zucchini until just tender; do not overcook. Scoop out pulp, leaving ½-inch shell if using large zucchini, ¼-inch shell if smaller zucchini. Reserve ¾ cup firmer part of pulp; chop. Saute mushrooms and onions in oil until soft. Add ½ cheese, along with eggs, rice, sunflower seeds, and reserved zucchini pulp. Stir in seasonings; heap mixture into zucchini shells. Top with remaining cheese. Bake at 325° for about 30 minutes in covered casserole dish. Sprinkle with parsley. Serves 4 as main dish, 6 as side dish.

Corn and Zucchini Pie

Pastry for 2-crust pie
Eggs 5, hard-cooked
Zucchini 1 cup coarsely chopped
Canned whole kernel corn 1½ cups drained
Flour 2 tablespoons
Cream ½ cup
Salt 1 teaspoon
White pepper ½ teaspoon
Milk 2 tablespoons

Line 10-inch Pyrex pie pan with pastry. Mix eggs, zucchini, and corn; spoon into crust. Mix flour with cream; season with salt and pepper. Pour over vegetables and cover with top crust. Crimp edges and slit crust. Brush crust with milk. Bake at 400° for 40 to 55 minutes until done and golden brown. Serves 6 as side dish.

Impossible Zucchini Pie

Zucchini   2 cups coarsely chopped
Onion   ⅔ cup chopped
Margarine or butter   1 tablespoon
Green chilies   1 3-ounce can
Cheddar cheese   1 cup shredded
Eggs   3
Milk   1½ cups
Buttermilk baking mix (biscuit mix)   ¾ cup
Salt   1 teaspoon
Fresh ground pepper   ½ teaspoon
Parmesan cheese   ¼ cup grated

Saute zucchini and onion in margarine until soft. Remove from heat; add green chilies and cheddar cheese. Place in greased 10-inch Pyrex pie plate. Place rest of ingredients, except parmesan, in blender. Cover and blend about 30 seconds on high speed. Pour over zucchini in pie plate. Sprinkle with parmesan cheese. Bake about 35 minutes at 400°, or until golden and center is set. Let stand about 5 minutes before cutting. Serves 4 generously, or 6 as side dish.

Baked Zucchini with Cream Sauce

Zucchini   2 medium, cut in ½-inch slices
Salt
White sauce   1½ cups, medium-thick
Parsley   1 tablespoon chopped
Chives   1 tablespoon chopped
Soft bread crumbs   1 cup
Butter   3 tablespoons
Basil   ¼ teaspoon
Oregano   ¼ teaspoon
Seasoned salt   ½ teaspoon

Steam zucchini slices until tender crisp; drain. Overlap slices in buttered casserole; salt lightly. Mix chopped parsley and chives into white sauce; spoon over zucchini. Saute bread crumbs in butter; mix in herbs and seasoning; sprinkle this topping over sauce. Bake at 350° for ½ hour. Serves 6.

Zucchini Tosca

Zucchini 4 cups peeled and cut up (can be firm flesh of large one)
Onion 1 medium, diced
Salt ½ teaspoon
Pepper ⅛ teaspoon
Pimento 3 tablespoons chopped
Soft bread crumbs 1½ cups
Margarine or butter ¼ cup
Condensed cream of mushroom soup 1 10¾-ounce can
Medium cheddar cheese ¼ cup shredded
Celery seed 1 tablespoon

Steam zucchini and onion until tender; mash. Add salt, pepper, and pimento; let drain in colander. Saute crumbs in butter. Alternate layers of zucchini, mushroom soup, and crumbs in buttered casserole or individual dishes. Repeat layers. Cover with cheddar cheese and sprinkle with celery seed. Bake at 350° for 25 minutes (20 minutes for individual dishes). Serves 6 as side dish.

Swiss Zucchini

Butter 3 tablespoons
Flour 3 tablespoons
Milk 1 cup, hot
Onion 1 tablespoon grated
Salt ¼ teaspoon
Zucchini 2 cups shredded (firm flesh of large one)
Vegetable oil 1 tablespoon
Eggs 2, hard-cooked and sliced
Salt and pepper to taste
Swiss cheese 1 cup shredded
Butter 1 tablespoon
Soft bread crumbs 3 tablespoons

Melt butter; add flour, stirring until it bubbles. Add hot milk slowly, stirring constantly until smooth. Add grated onion and salt; cook 5 minutes, stirring. Saute shredded zucchini in oil slowly for 10 minutes, stirring. Stir in thick cream sauce and sliced eggs. Add salt and pepper to taste.

Transfer half this mixture to buttered casserole. Top with half of swiss cheese, then add rest of creamed zucchini. Top with the rest of swiss cheese; sprinkle with buttered crumbs. Bake at 400° for 15 minutes, until top is browned and bubbly. Serves 4 to 6.

Zucchini Souffle

Zucchini   3 medium, peeled and sliced
Butter   1 tablespoon melted
Onion   2 tablespoons grated
Salt   1 teaspoon
Sugar   ⅛ teaspoon
Fresh ground pepper
Eggs   3, separated
Fresh soft bread crumbs   ¼ cup

Steam zucchini until very tender; drain in cheesecloth-lined colander; squeeze out excess juice. Mash and beat until smooth; drain again in colander. Add butter, onion, salt, sugar, pepper, and egg yolks. Mix well and beat. Fold in 3 stiffly-beaten egg whites. Spoon carefully into individual oiled souffle molds. Sprinkle with crumbs. Bake at 375° for 25 minutes or until set and puffed. Serve at once. Serves 4.

Company Souffle Omelet

Butter   3 tablespoons
Flour   4 tablespoons
Milk   1 cup, hot
Onion   1 tablespoon grated
Salt   ¼ teaspoon
Eggs   3, separated
Zucchini   2 cups, any size, peeled and cubed. This makes about 1 cup
   when steamed and mashed.
Salt and pepper   to taste
Soft bread crumbs   3 tablespoons, buttered

Melt butter; add flour; stir until it bubbles. Add hot milk slowly, stirring constantly until smooth. Add grated onion and salt; cook 5 minutes, stirring. Pour this into beaten egg yolks; mix. Steam zucchini until tender, about 15 to 20 minutes depending on maturity of squash and size of cubes. Drain in colander; mash; drain again. Add mashed zucchini to cream sauce, season to taste, and cool. Fold in stiffly beaten egg whites. Transfer mixture to large buttered iron skillet or casserole. Sprinkle with buttered crumbs; bake in preheated 350° oven for 35 to 40 minutes, or until firm and set. Loosen edges; turn out onto hot platter. Serves 4.

Easy Omelet

Zucchini   1 medium, sliced
Onion   ½ small, chopped
Green pepper   ½, chopped
Vegetable oil   2 tablespoons
Potato   1 small, boiled and diced
Eggs   4
Salt and pepper   to taste

Saute zucchini, onion, and green pepper in oil until zucchini is barely tender. Add diced potato. Beat eggs lightly and season; pour over vegetables and cook slowly until firm. Turn out onto hot plate; cut into wedges. Serves 4.

A hearty brunch for Sunday morning.

Baked Omelet

Zucchini   2 cups peeled and cubed (can be firm flesh of very large one)
Onion   ½, grated
Eggs   5, beaten
Medium cheddar cheese   ½ cup shredded
Fresh ground pepper
Seasoned salt   to taste
Parsley   1 tablespoon chopped
Cracker crumbs or dry bread crumbs   4 tablespoons

Steam zucchini cubes until tender; mash and drain in colander. Combine with rest of ingredients, except crumbs. Pour into greased pan; top with crumbs. Bake at 350° for 45 minutes or until completely set. Serves 4.

Zucchini Oven Frittata

Zucchini 2½ cups thinly sliced
Green onions 2, finely sliced
Cooking oil 1 tablespoon
Eggs 7
Fresh parsley 2 tablespoons chopped
Parmesan cheese ¾ cup grated
Seasoning salt ½ teaspoon
Oregano 1 teaspoon

Saute zucchini and onions in oil until softened; set aside. Beat eggs with all remaining ingredients except oregano. Add zucchini and onions; pour into greased 9 × 9-inch baking pan. Sprinkle with oregano. Bake 25 to 30 minutes at 350°, or until firm. Let stand at least 5 minutes before cutting. Good either warm or chilled. Can be cut into small squares for appetizer. Serves 6.

Golden Broil

Yellow or green zucchini 3 medium
Vegetable oil
Margarine ¼ cup, softened
Parmesan cheese ½ cup grated
Onion 1 tablespoon grated
Potato chips 3 tablespoons crushed
Salt and pepper to taste

Slice zucchini lengthwise in ¼-inch-thick slices. Saute each in oil for several minutes on each side; remove to broiler pan. Combine margarine, cheese, onion, potato chips; spread on tops of slices and season to taste. Broil until bubbly and browned. Serves 4 to 6 as side dish.

Zucchini Scallop

Zucchini 3 medium, cut in ½-inch slices
Garlic clove 1, crushed
Mayonnaise ½ cup
Soft bread crumbs ½ cup
Medium cheddar or swiss cheese ½ cup grated
Celery seed ½ teaspoon

Put zucchini slices in buttered casserole or 9 × 13 × 2-inch pan. Mix crushed garlic into mayonnaise; spread over zucchini slices. Bake at 350° for 20 minutes. Combine bread crumbs and cheese; scatter evenly over top; sprinkle with celery seed. Bake at 350° for 20 minutes more or until zucchini is tender.

Very good as leftovers.

Medley of Vegetables

Eggplant   1 medium, peeled and cut in ½-inch slices
Zucchini   2 medium, cut in ½-inch slices
Eggs   2, beaten
Butter
Cream cheese   1 3-ounce package
Beer Sauce
Monterey jack cheese   3 large slices
Cheddar cheese   4 ounces, sliced

Dip eggplant and zucchini in egg and saute in butter approximately 5 minutes on each side. Place layer of eggplant in casserole; top with cream cheese and layer of zucchini; cover with Beer Sauce. Continue layering, substituting monterey jack and cheddar cheese (reserve last slice of each) for cream cheese. Top each layer with Beer Sauce; then put last slices of monterey jack and cheddar cheeses on top. Place uncovered in oven and bake at 350° for 45 to 50 minutes. Makes 6 servings.

Beer Sauce

Condensed tomato soup   1 10¾-ounce can
Mushrooms   1 3-ounce can, sliced and drained
Stewed tomatoes   1 14½-ounce can
Beer   ½ cup
Tomato paste   1 6-ounce can
Green pepper   ½, diced
Onion   1 medium, diced
Oregano   2 teaspoons
Basil   ½ teaspoon
Salt   1 teaspoon

Combine all ingredients in saucepan. Bring to a boil and simmer 5 minutes.

Make-Ahead Zucchini Strata

Bread   10 to 12 slices stale or "day-old"
Zucchini   1½ cups coarsely chopped
Onion   ½ cup chopped
Margarine   2 tablespoons
Cheddar cheese   1 cup shredded
Eggs   6
Milk   1 cup
Small curd cottage cheese   2 cups
White pepper   ½ teaspoon
Salt   to taste

Cube bread and layer ⅔ of cubes in bottom of oiled 9 × 13-inch baking pan. Saute zucchini and onion in margarine, layer on top of bread, then cover with shredded cheese. Layer remaining bread cubes over top. Beat eggs with milk; stir in cottage cheese and pepper. Salt to taste. Pour egg mixture over strata ingredients, cover with foil, and refrigerate for several hours or overnight. Remove from refrigerator about an hour before baking. Bake uncovered 50 to 60 minutes at 350°. If it browns too quickly, cover with foil. Serves 6 to 8. **Note:**   For a meaty main dish, add chicken, tuna, sausage, or other meat along with the zucchini layer.

Stove-Top Casserole

Zucchini   4 cups sliced (can be from large one, center pulp discarded)
Vegetable oil   3 tablespoons
Garlic cloves   2, crushed
Salt and freshly ground pepper
Spaghetti sauce   1 16-ounce can, heated
Mozzarella cheese   ¾ pound, thinly sliced
Oregano   1 teaspoon crushed
Basil   ¼ teaspoon

In large Teflon skillet saute zucchini slices 1 cup at a time, in 1 tablespoon oil, with garlic. Cook until almost tender and a little brown; drain on paper towels. Pour off any excess oil; then layer hot zucchini in skillet, seasoning lightly with salt and pepper, and spreading each layer with some of the hot spaghetti sauce and sliced mozzarella cheese. Cover top layer with cheese and sprinkle with herbs. Cover and cook very slowly until mixture is just bubbly and cheese is melted. Serves 6.

Blender Casserole

Zucchini 4 cups sliced (can be thawed slices of frozen zucchini)
Eggs 3
Seasoned salt 1 teaspoon
Freshly ground pepper ½ teaspoon
Worcestershire sauce ½ teaspoon
Bran ¼ cup
Wheat germ ¼ cup
Buttered crumbs ½ cup
Mushrooms ½ pound, sliced
Onions ¼ cup finely chopped
Cheddar cheese ½ cup shredded
Paprika

Put zucchini in blender container with eggs, salt, pepper, and worcestershire sauce. Blend. Stir in bran and wheat germ. Put ½ of the buttered crumbs in the bottom of a large shallow oiled casserole. Pour in half zucchini mixture. Layer on half of the mushrooms and all of the chopped onions. Cover with the rest of the zucchini mixture. Layer remaining mushrooms over mixture. Top with crumbs and shredded cheese. Sprinkle heavily with paprika. Bake at 350° for 25 minutes. Check for doneness. If casserole shape is deep instead of shallow, it may take 30 minutes to bake. Serves 6.

Twenty-Minute Casserole

Zucchini 3 cups sliced (medium-sized zucchini)
Red onion 1 large, sliced and separated into rings
Green chilies 1 3-ounce can
Jack cheese 1½ cups shredded
Seasoning salt 1 teaspoon, or to taste
Ritz cracker crumbs ½ cup
Eggs 3, beaten
Dairy sour cream ½ cup

Steam zucchini slices and onion rings about 5 minutes. Place ½ in buttered shallow Pyrex casserole. Top with ½ chilies, cheese, seasoning, and cracker crumbs; repeat layers. Top with beaten eggs and bake, covered, at 350° for about 20 minutes, or until eggs are firm. Spread with sour cream and serve at once. Serves 6.

Quick Cheese Casserole

Zucchini   2 medium, thinly sliced
Onion   1, sliced and separated into rings
Tomatoes   3, sliced (or 1 14½-ounce can tomatoes, drained)
Celery   1 cup thinly sliced
Frozen peas   ½ 10-ounce package
Onion salt   ⅛ teaspoon
Fresh ground pepper   ¼ teaspoon
Condensed cheese soup   1 10¾-ounce can
Paprika

Mix vegetables with onion salt and pepper; put in greased casserole. Bake at 325° for 15 minutes. Spread cheese soup on top; sprinkle with paprika. Bake until zucchini is tender and cheese is bubbly. Serves 4.

Last-Minute Casserole

Zucchini   about 3 pounds medium, cut in ½-inch slices
Onion   1 cup chopped
Green pepper   ½ cup chopped
Golden mushroom soup   1 10¾-ounce can
Milk   ½ cup
Cracker crumbs   1 cup
Seasoning salt   to taste
Cheddar cheese   ½ cup shredded
Margarine or butter   2 tablespoons, melted

Steam zucchini slices, or boil about 5 minutes in small amount of water, drain, and set aside. Saute onion and green pepper. Combine all ingredients except shredded cheese and margarine. Pour mixture into greased 8 × 8-inch pan and sprinkle with cheese. Bake for about ½ hour at 350°. Drizzle with melted margarine or butter. Serves 4 generously, or 6 as side dish.

Egg Foo Yung

Eggs 3
Onion 1 small, grated
Bean sprouts ½ cup
Zucchini 1 cup unpeeled and grated, drained in colander
Wheat germ ½ cup
Salt ½ teaspoon
Vegetable oil
Rice cooked

Beat eggs until thick and lemon colored. Stir in rest of ingredients except oil and rice. Drop from tablespoon onto hot, oiled griddle. Brown on one side; turn and brown other side. Serve with Sweet and Sour Sauce and fluffy rice.

Sweet and Sour Sauce

Frozen apple juice ¼ cup, undiluted
Catsup 1 tablespoon
Cornstarch 2 teaspoons
Soy sauce 1 tablespoon
Vinegar ¼ cup

Heat apple juice and catsup together. Dissolve cornstarch in soy sauce and vinegar; add to apple juice. Simmer until thick and clear.

Entrees with
Meat, Poultry, or Fish

Zucchini Tacos

Vegetable oil   1 teaspoon
Lean ground beef   ¼ pound
Onion   1 small, finely chopped
Zucchini   1 medium, diced
Green chilies   ¼ cup chopped (optional)
Tomatoes   2, quartered
Taco sauce   1 cup
Taco shells
Yellow cheese   grated
Lettuce   shredded
Onion   sliced

Heat oil in skillet; add crumbled ground beef and cook until meat loses its pink color. Drain off fat. Add onion, zucchini, green chilies, and tomatoes. Cook slowly until zucchini is tender. Add taco sauce; reheat. Serve in heated taco shells garnished with cheese, lettuce, and onion. Serves 4.

Bette's Bella Zucchini

Zucchini   1 medium large (8 to 10 inches)
Olive oil   2 tablespoons
Ground beef   ½ pound
Ham   ½ cup diced
Onion   1 small, chopped
Parsley   2 tablespoons chopped
Oregano leaves   ½ teaspoon crumbled
Salt and pepper   to taste
Tomato sauce   2 tablespoons
Fine bread crumbs   ⅔ cup
Butter   2 tablespoons, melted
Parmesan cheese   grated

Split zucchini lengthwise; scoop out all of center pulp and seeds; chop and put aside. Saute beef, ham, and onion in olive oil; add rest of ingredients except butter and cheese. Mix in pulp; pile into scooped-out centers, top with butter and parmesan cheese. Bake at 350° for 1 hour or until tender. Serves 2 to 4.

Mother's Casserole

Ground beef or lamb   1 pound
Onion   1, chopped
Tomatoes   1 28-ounce can, drain and reserve liquid
Green pepper   1 small, cut in strips
Zucchini   6 medium, thickly sliced
Medium cheddar cheese   ¾ cup shredded
Flour   2 tablespoons
Ripe olives   ½ cup sliced
Garlic clove   1, crushed
Salt   1 teaspoon
Oregano   ¼ teaspoon
Parmesan cheese   grated
Paprika

Sprinkle salt on hot Teflon* skillet; add meat and onion; saute until meat is light brown and crumbly. Drain off extra fat. Add drained tomatoes, green pepper strips, and zucchini slices; saute 10 minutes. Add reserved tomato liquid mixed with 2 tablespoons flour, cheese, olives, garlic, and seasoning. Reheat for a minute; then spoon into casserole. Sprinkle thickly with the parmesan cheese and paprika. Bake at 350° for 1 hour until thick and browned. Serves 6 to 8.

* If not using Teflon, use 1 tablespoon vegetable oil.

Beer Barrel Stew

Beer 2 cups
Beef stock or beef bouillon ½ cup
Onions 2 large, sliced
Beef chuck 2 pounds, cut in bite-size pieces
Carrots 3 large, diced
Mushrooms ½ cup sliced
Celery 1 stalk, sliced
Zucchini 2 medium, sliced
Turnip 1, cubed
Salt and pepper to taste
Nutmeg pinch
Powdered lemon peel ¼ teaspoon
Powdered bay leaf ¼ teaspoon
Mild cheddar cheese ½ cup shredded
Potatoes 2 cups mashed, hot
Parsley 2 tablespoons chopped

Boil beer to reduce it to half; add beef stock. Spread onions in large dutch oven; cover with layers of beef chuck and top with layer of vegetables mixed together, sprinkling with salt and pepper. Add nutmeg, lemon peel, and bay leaf to hot beer liquid; pour over mixture in pot. Cover tightly and bake at 350° for 4 to 4½ hours. Stir cheese into mashed potatoes; spoon around outer edge of hot stew. Broil, uncovered, until potatoes are lightly browned. Sprinkle with parsley. Serves 6 to 8.

Zucchini with Meat Balls

Zucchini 1 very large
Tomatoes 1 28-ounce can
Tomato sauce 1 8-ounce can
Worcestershire sauce 1 teaspoon
Ground lamb or beef 1 pound
Egg 1
Rice 1 cup cooked
Onion ½ cup finely chopped
Salt ½ teaspoon
Fresh ground pepper ¼ teaspoon
Fresh mint leaves 1 tablespoon chopped (with lamb)
Fresh dill leaves 1 tablespoon chopped (with beef)

Cut zucchini in quarters lengthwise; scoop out center pulp; put pulp in large skillet with tomatoes, tomato sauce, and worcestershire sauce. Mix rest of ingredients except zucchini and form into small meat balls. Heat tomato mixture to simmering; drop in meat balls; simmer slowly for 15 minutes, covered. Slice zucchini quarters in half lengthwise; cut into thin slices; add to simmering meat balls. Cover and cook slowly until zucchini is tender. Serves 4.

Swiss Steak with Invisible Zucchini

Round steak 2 pounds, cut in serving-size pieces
Flour ½ cup
Vegetable oil 2 tablespoons
Salt and pepper to taste
Zucchini 3 cups peeled and diced (can be firm flesh of very large one)
Onion 1, sliced
Celery 4 stalks, sliced
Green pepper 1, cut in chunks
Tomatoes 2 cups cooked or canned (optional)

Place round steak on floured cutting board, cover with flour and pound it into meat; turn and do the same. Brown pieces in hot oil; season to taste; pour off any excess oil. Turn down heat; put diced zucchini around steak pieces; cover with sliced vegetables. Cook slowly for 3 hours or until steak is fork tender. Zucchini will provide needed moisture for slow cooking. 2 cups cooked (or canned) tomatoes may be added; any extra juice can be evaporated at end of cooking time by simmering uncovered. Serves 4.

Chard-Stuffed Zucchini

Zucchini 1 large, cut in half lengthwise
Vegetable oil
Swiss chard 2 cups cooked and chopped
Ground beef or lamb 1 pound
Onion 1, finely chopped
Condensed tomato soup ½ 10¾-ounce can
Pepper ¼ teaspoon
Thyme ½ teaspoon
Salt ¾ teaspoon
Soft bread 4 slices, cubed
Parsley 3 tablespoons chopped
Parmesan cheese ¼ cup grated
Eggs 2, beaten

Scoop out seeds and pulp from center of zucchini halves; discard. Score zucchini flesh in 1-inch squares and rub with oil. Cook swiss chard until tender; drain well and chop finely.

Sprinkle salt in hot Teflon* skillet; brown meat and onion. Drain off fat. Add tomato soup and seasonings; simmer 5 minutes to blend flavors. Stir in rest of ingredients; mix well. Fill centers of zucchini halves with mixture, pressing into place. Bake in shallow oiled pan or on cookie sheet at 325° for about 1 hour or until zucchini is tender. Cut in crosswise slices. Serves 8.
* If not using Teflon, add 1 tablespoon vegetable oil.

Stuffed Zucchini Fingers

Zucchini   12 small (or more)
Vegetable oil   2 tablespoons
Meat Stuffing
Yogurt Sauce

Hollow out zucchini with apple corer (if longer than 3 inches, cut into 3-inch lengths). Stuff with meat mixture; saute in oil for 10 minutes, turning gently. Place in shallow greased casserole, top with sauce, and bake at 350° for ½ hour.

Meat Stuffing

Ground beef or lamb   ¾ pound
Onion   1, finely chopped
Wheat germ   ¼ cup
Egg   1, beaten
Salt and pepper   to taste

Saute meat and onion until meat loses its red color. Cool; add wheat germ, beaten egg, and seasoning; mix.

Yogurt Sauce

Cornstarch   2 teaspoons
Yogurt   1 pint
Garlic salt   ½ teaspoon
Oregano   ½ teaspoon, if using beef
Mint   ½ teaspoon, crushed, if using lamb

Mix cornstarch with half of yogurt; stir into the other half and add seasonings. Heat on low until piping hot; pour over zucchini fingers and bake.

Zucchini a la Maddalena

Zucchini   3 large
Ground beef   1 pound
Bread crumbs   ½ cup
Parmesan cheese   ¼ cup grated
Egg   1
Salt and pepper   to taste
Parsley
Vegetable oil
Tomato sauce   1 8-ounce can

Parboil zucchini. Split lengthwise into 4 parts; remove pulp; squeeze out excess water. Add pulp to ground beef, bread crumbs, cheese and egg; add salt, pepper, and parsley to taste; mix well.

Sprinkle zucchini shells with salt and place in baking dish that is at least 1 inch deep. Brush shells lightly with oil; fill with meat mixture. Dilute tomato sauce with ½ can of water and pour over and around zucchini. Bake at 350° for 1 hour. While baking, baste zucchini with drippings. Make sure pan always has at least ½-inch liquid around shells, adding more water if necessary.

Noodle Casserole

Ground beef 1 pound
Tomato sauce 2 8-ounce cans
Oregano ½ teaspoon
Zucchini 3 cups sliced
Salt
Wide noodles 8 ounces
Cottage cheese 1 cup
Cream cheese 4 ounces, softened
Fresh ground pepper ⅛ teaspoon
Green onions 4, finely chopped
Yogurt or dairy sour cream ¼ cup

Cook beef in skillet until meat loses its red color; drain off fat. Add oregano, tomato sauce, and zucchini. Simmer 5 minutes; add salt to taste. In the meantime, cook noodles in salted water until tender; drain. Put half of noodles in shallow greased baking dish. Mix 1 teaspoon salt, cottage cheese, cream cheese, pepper, green onions, and yogurt or sour cream. Spread this on noodles; add remaining noodles. Pour meat-zucchini mixture over top. Bake in moderate oven (350°) about 30 minutes. Serves 6.

Good also when reheated.

Potato Pot

Zucchini   3 cups sliced
Onion   ¼ cup minced
Margarine   ¼ cup
Roast beef, lamb, or pork   2 cups diced
Potatoes   6 medium, cooked and diced
Milk   ½ cup
Dry red wine   ½ cup
Soy sauce   2 tablespoons
Parsley   2 tablespoons chopped
Thyme   ¼ teaspoon
Marjoram   ¼ teaspoon
Salt and pepper   to taste
Paprika   ½ teaspoon

Saute zucchini and onion in margarine for 2 to 3 minutes. Add remaining ingredients, except paprika; mix well. Put in large casserole and sprinkle with paprika. Bake at 350° for 45 minutes, basting occasionally with liquid of casserole. When cooked, thicken if necessary. To thicken pour off ¼ cup liquid; cool in saucepan and mix in 1 tablespoon flour. Pour off rest of hot liquid into saucepan; simmer, stirring until thickened and smooth. Pour back over casserole. Serves 6.

Goulash

Elbow macaroni   8 ounces
Ground beef   1 pound
Onion   1, chopped
Zucchini   3 cups sliced
Frozen peas   ½ 10-ounce package, thawed
Tomatoes   1 7½-ounce can, drain and reserve liquid
Flour   1 tablespoon
Salt   2 teaspoons
Fresh ground pepper   ½ teaspoon
Condensed tomato soup   1 10¾-ounce can
Soft bread crumbs   ½ cup
Margarine   2 tablespoons, melted

Cook and drain macaroni. Cook beef and onion in hot salted Teflon skillet until meat loses its red color. Drain off fat. Add zucchini slices, thawed peas, and tomatoes; saute 5 minutes, stirring gently. Add tomato liquid mixed with flour, cooked macaroni, seasonings, and tomato soup. Mix well and heat through. Pour into 2-quart shallow casserole. Mix bread crumbs with melted margarine; sprinkle on top of mixture. Bake at 350° approximately 26 minutes. Serves 6 to 8.

Danish Zucchini Goulash

Beef stew meat   1 pound, cubed
Vegetable oil   1 tablespoon
Salt   2 teaspoons
Fresh ground pepper   ½ teaspoon
Ground bay leaves   ½ teaspoon
Zucchini   5 cups peeled and cubed (can be from very large one)
Onion   1, coarsely chopped
Frozen apple juice   ¼ cup, thawed but not diluted
Flour   1 tablespoon
Paprika   1 tablespoon
Vinegar   1 tablespoon
Frozen apple juice   2 tablespoons, undiluted
Dairy sour cream   ½ cup
Noodles   4 cups cooked and buttered

Brown beef cubes in hot oil; add seasonings, 3 cups zucchini, onion, and ¼ cup apple juice. Simmer slowly, covered, for 2 to 3 hours or until meat is very tender. Cubed zucchini will cook up and form thick juice around meat. 15 minutes before serving, mix in remaining zucchini; cook 5 minutes, covered. Mix flour and paprika with vinegar and 2 tablespoons apple juice; stir this into cooking meat sauce. Stir and simmer 10 minutes until zucchini is barely tender and sauce well thickened. Stir in sour cream just before serving. Good on buttered noodles. Serves 4 to 6.

Zucchini Shepherd Pie

Beef stew meat*   1 pound, precooked until tender
Onions   2, coarsely chopped and sauteed
Carrots   4 large, cut in chunks, cooked until tender
Mushrooms   ½ pound, sliced (or 1 4-ounce can stems and pieces)
Zucchini   1½ cups sliced and steamed until tender
Meat gravy   2 cups
Mashed potatoes   3 cups

Combine meat, onions, carrots, mushrooms, zucchini, and gravy in large casserole. Top with mashed potatoes, spreading potatoes around edges of casserole, leaving hole in center for gravy to bubble up. (If you are assembling hot meat–gravy mixture and hot mashed potatoes, you can just put this under the broiler long enough to brown top of potatoes.) If prepared earlier in the day and refrigerated, bake at 350° until hot and bubbly and potatoes are tipped with golden brown, about 1 hour. Serves 8.
* You can use instead 1 pound of ground beef, browned, or 1½ to 2 cups of leftover cooked beef roast.

Zucchini-Stuffed Steaks

Jack cheese   4 thin slices
Zucchini   4 small (approximately 4-inch size)
Cube steaks   4
Seasoning salt   to taste
Bacon   8 slices
Cooking oil   2 teaspoons
Chicken bouillon   2 cubes
Boiling water   1½ cups
Onion   ½ cup chopped
Flour   2 tablespoons, mixed into ¾ cup cold water

Place one slice cheese and one small zucchini on each cube steak. Sprinkle with seasoning salt. Roll up each steak; wrap with two slices of bacon, side by side, and skewer with toothpicks to hold in place. Brown steaks in oil, turning evenly. Add bouillon dissolved in boiling water. Add onion. Simmer steak roll-ups until tender. Lift them out of liquid. Add flour mixture and simmer, stirring, until thick (about 20 to 30 minutes). Replace steaks and reheat as necessary. Serves 4.

Meat Loaf

Zucchini   2 medium, chopped (or 3 cups large chopped zucchini)
Onions   2 small, chopped
Tomatoes   2, chopped (or 1 7½-ounce can tomatoes, drained)
Vegetable oil   1 tablespoon
Egg   1
Worcestershire sauce   1 tablespoon
Garlic clove   1, crushed
Salt   1 teaspoon
Fresh ground pepper   ½ teaspoon
Sage   ½ teaspoon
Soft bread crumbs   ½ cup
Ground beef   1½ pounds

Saute zucchini, onions, and tomatoes in oil; simmer until tender. Cool, drain, and mash. Beat egg; stir in worcestershire sauce, garlic, seasonings, and mashed vegetables. Add bread crumbs and ground beef; mix well. Let stand at room temperature for ½ hour; then pack into oiled loaf pan, mound up top, and bake at 325° for 1½ hours. Drain off accumulated fat. Let stand at room temperature for 15 minutes before slicing. Serves 8.

Moussaka Casserole

Ground lamb or beef   1 pound
Onions   2, chopped
Tomatoes   4, chopped (or 1 14½-ounce can tomatoes, drained)
Red wine   ¼ cup
Fresh ground pepper   ⅛ teaspoon
Cinnamon   ⅛ teaspoon
Parsley   3 tablespoons chopped
Thyme   pinch
Salt   to taste
Eggplant   1 medium, peeled and cut in ½-inch-thick slices
Zucchini   2 medium, cut in ½-inch-thick slices
Vegetable oil
Cottage cheese   1 cup, drained (or dry curd)
White sauce   1½ cups, medium-thick
Soft bread crumbs   ½ cup
Parmesan cheese   ¾ cup grated

Heat large Teflon skillet; sprinkle with salt; add meat and onions; stir fry until meat starts to brown. Add tomatoes, wine, pepper, cinnamon, parsley, and thyme. Simmer until thick and liquid has cooked out, stirring occasionally. Add salt to taste. Saute eggplant and zucchini slices in oil until almost tender. Add cottage cheese to white sauce. In buttered 9 × 13-inch pan or large casserole, layer the eggplant on the bottom. Combine bread crumbs and parmesan; sprinkle half of it on the eggplant; top with half of meat mixture. On top of this layer zucchini slices; sprinkle with rest of bread crumbs and parmesan, and rest of meat mixture. Top with white sauce mixture. Bake at 350° for 1 hour or until bubbly and browned. Let casserole stand for 15 minutes or more before serving. Serves 6.

Spaghetti Sauce

Salt   ½ teaspoon
Ground beef   ½ pound
Mushrooms   ½ pound, sliced (or 1 4-ounce can mushroom stems
    and pieces)
Green pepper   1, chopped
Tomatoes   2, quartered
Garlic clove   1, minced (or ½ chopped onion)
Red wine   ½ cup
Condensed tomato soup   1 10¾-ounce can
Oregano   ½ teaspoon
Thyme   pinch
Basil   pinch
Sugar   ¼ teaspoon
Zucchini   2 medium, cut in half lengthwise, then cut crosswise in thin slices
Salt and pepper   to taste

Saute ground beef in hot salted Teflon skillet until lightly browned; pour off most of fat. Add mushrooms, green pepper, tomatoes, and garlic or onion, and saute a few minutes longer. Add wine, tomato soup, herbs, and sugar; stir. Simmer ½ hour to blend flavors. Add thin zucchini slices; simmer until zucchini is tender. Salt and pepper as necessary. This makes a nice thick sauce. Serves 4.

Zucchini Lasagna

Onion   ½ cup finely chopped
Garlic   1 clove, minced
Olive oil   2 tablespoons
Ground beef   1 pound
Tomato sauce   1 8-ounce can
Tomato paste   1 6-ounce can
Water   ¾ cup
Mushrooms   1 2-ounce can, sliced
Italian seasoning   ¾ teaspoon
Salt   2 teaspoons
Egg   1, beaten
Zucchini   2 cups grated
Cottage cheese   2 cups
Parmesan cheese   ¼ cup grated
Lasagna noodles   1 8-ounce package
Mozzarella cheese   ½ pound, sliced

Saute onion and garlic in oil. Add ground beef and cook until brown. Add tomato sauce, tomato paste, water, mushrooms with liquid, italian seasoning, and 1 teaspoon salt. Simmer uncovered 15 to 20 minutes.

Combine beaten egg, zucchini, cottage cheese, parmesan cheese, and remaining 1 teaspoon salt.

Cook lasagna in boiling salted water until tender (about 10 minutes). Place in colander under running cold water and drain on paper towels.

Pour ½ of the meat sauce in bottom of 9 × 13-inch pan. Cover with layer of lasagna (6 noodles, overlapping), ½ the zucchini mixture, another layer of noodles, ½ the cheese slices, the rest of the zucchini mixture, final layer of noodles, the rest of the meat mixture, and top with cheese.

Cover and bake at 375° for 30 minutes. Uncover and bake 10 minutes more. Makes 8 to 10 servings.

Reprinted from the Seattle Post-Intelligencer *by permission of Louis Guzzo.*

Double Zucchini Lasagna

Following previous recipe, replace lasagna noodles with 18 thin slices of zucchini, prepared as follows: cut off each end of 6- or 8-inch-long zucchini.

Then slice lengthways in ⅛-inch slices. Sprinkle slices with salt, put between several thicknesses of paper towels, and weight down with heavy plate for 1 hour. Use 6 slices of zucchini instead of each noodle layer. Bake as directed.

Eccedenza Diletto ("leftover delight")

Water 2 cups
Oil or butter 1 teaspoon
Chicken seasoned stock base 2 teaspoons
Rice 1 cup
Butter or margarine 4 tablespoons
Zucchini 3 small, thinly sliced
Onion 1 cup chopped
Whole kernel corn 1 8-ounce can, drained (or leftover fresh corn cut
    from the cob)
Tomatoes 1 1-pound can, cut in quarters
Salt 1½ teaspoons
Pepper ¼ teaspoon
Ground coriander seed 1 teaspoon
Leaf oregano 1 teaspoon
Leftover lamb roast 3 to 4 cups cooked, cut in cubes
Leftover vegetables if desired
Tomato sauce 1 8-ounce can
Butter or margarine 4 tablespoons
Curry powder ¾ teaspoon
Bread 3 slices, cubed or crumbled

Put water in saucepan. Add oil and chicken stock base. Bring to a boil, stir in rice and cook according to package directions. Melt butter in skillet and saute onion and zucchini until almost tender.

Pour rice in a large greased casserole. Add zucchini and onion. Add corn, tomatoes and juice, salt, pepper, coriander, oregano, meat, and leftover vegetables, if desired. Add enough tomato sauce to moisten.

Melt butter in skillet. Stir in curry. Add bread cubes and mix well. Sprinkle over top of casserole. Bake at 350° for 20 to 25 minutes or until heated through. Serves 8 to 10.

Recipe by Ruth deRosa, reprinted from the Seattle Times.

Slow Cookery Pork Chops and Zucchini

Zucchini   3 small, cut in ¼-inch slices
Pork chops   4
Fresh ground pepper
Garlic powder
Chicken bouillon cube   1
Hot water   3 tablespoons
Basil   ¼ teaspoon
Oregano   ¼ teaspoon
Flour   to thicken juice, if desired
Cooked rice

Slice zucchini into bottom of slow cookery pot. Trim fat from pork chops. Rub hot frying pan with trimmed pork fat; discard fat. Brown the pork chops on both sides in frying pan. Season with pepper and garlic powder. Drain off any excess fat. Transfer pork chops to slow cooker. Dissolve bouillon in water, pour over pork chops and zucchini. Sprinkle with herbs. Cook ½ hour on high, then turn to low and cook 6 to 8 hours. Juice can be thickened with flour to serve on rice.

Stuffed Zucchini Rings

Zucchini   4 1½-inch-thick slices from very large one
Brown rice   1 cup freshly cooked
Medium cheddar cheese   ⅓ cup grated
Ham, chicken, or leftover meat   ½ cup minced
Seasoned salt   ½ teaspoon
Red wine   ¼ cup
Fresh ground pepper
Paprika
Red wine   ¼ cup, for basting

Cut across zucchini in 1½-inch slices; do not peel. Remove center pulp and seeds; discard, leaving large rings for stuffing. Put these on greased baking sheet or in shallow pan. Combine all ingredients except paprika and wine; fill centers of rings. Sprinkle generously with paprika. Bake at 350° for 35 minutes or until zucchini is tender, basting twice. Serves 4.

Refreshing Oven Stew

Frozen mixed vegetables 1 10-ounce package
Potato 1 small, peeled and cubed
Water ¼ cup
Vegetable bouillon cube 1
Worcestershire sauce 1 teaspoon
Soy sauce 2 tablespoons
Tomatoes 2, quartered
Cauliflower or broccoli flowerets 1 cup
Zucchini 2 medium, sliced
Onion 1 small, chopped
Leftover meat 1 cup cubed (or ½ cup slivered lunch meat)
Seasoned salt 1 teaspoon
Oregano ¼ teaspoon
Sage pinch

In dutch oven with lid, simmer frozen mixed vegetables and potato cubes for 5 minutes in water with bouillon, worcestershire, and soy sauce added. Add rest of vegetables, meat, and seasonings. Cover and bake at 350° for 40 minutes or until vegetables are tender. Juice can be poured off and thickened for thicker stew. Serves 4.

Stew can be cooked on top of stove, but cook very slowly, covered; stir occasionally, checking to be sure it does not cook dry.

Ham Lunch

Margarine 2 tablespoons, softened
Butter flavoring ¼ teaspoon
Zucchini 3 cups sliced
Mushrooms ½ pound, sliced
Green onions 2 cups thinly sliced
Pressed ham luncheon meat 1 5-ounce package, slivered
Seasoned salt ½ teaspoon
Freshly ground pepper ¼ teaspoon
Romano cheese grated, to garnish

Add butter flavoring to margarine in fry pan or wok. Saute zucchini, mushrooms, and green onions until barely tender. Stir in ham and seasonings; saute until ham is heated through. Serve garnished with cheese. Serves 3 or 4.

Zucchini Tetrazzini

Zucchini   3 cups diced (can be firm flesh of very large one)
Salt
Ham   2 cups cooked, cut in strips
Mushrooms   ½ pound, sliced
Margarine   ¼ cup, softened
Onion   1 small, diced
Flour   ¼ cup
Chicken bouillon   1 cup, hot
Milk   1 cup
Swiss cheese   ⅓ cup shredded
Dry mustard   ½ teaspoon
Fresh ground pepper   ⅛ teaspoon
Parmesan cheese   ⅓ cup grated
Slivered almonds   optional

Steam zucchini until barely tender; salt lightly; drain and keep warm. In large saucepan, saute ham and mushrooms in margarine about 3 minutes; remove and keep warm. Saute onions until golden, then blend in flour. Gradually add bouillon and milk; cook over low heat, stirring, until thick and smooth. Add swiss cheese, mustard, and pepper; stir until cheese melts. Add ham and mushrooms; stir in drained zucchini. Spoon into shallow buttered casserole; sprinkle with parmesan cheese and scatter almonds on top. Broil until light brown and bubbly. Serves 6.

Macaroni con Zucchini

Elbow macaroni 1 8-ounce package
Onion 1 large, chopped
Vegetable oil 1 tablespoon
Zucchini 2½ cups diced (can be from large one)
Mushrooms ¼ pound, sliced
Ripe olives ¼ cup sliced
Margarine 2 tablespoons
French dressing ¼ cup
Medium process cheese ¼ cup shredded
Parmesan cheese ¼ cup grated
Milk 3 tablespoons
Pastrami ¼ pound sliced, cut in strips
Oregano ¼ teaspoon crushed
Fresh ground pepper ⅛ teaspoon
Salt to taste
Paprika

Boil macaroni in salted water until tender; drain. Saute onion in oil; stir into macaroni. Saute rest of vegetables in margarine and french dressing until zucchini is barely tender. Add to macaroni with cheeses, milk, pastrami, and seasonings. Mix; turn into shallow casserole. Sprinkle with paprika; bake at 350° for 20 minutes. Serves 6.

Very good reheated.

Ruthie's Zucchini Pizza

Zucchini 3 cups grated, drained, and pressed dry between paper towels
Eggs 3, beaten
Flour ⅔ cup
Salt ½ teaspoon
Parmesan cheese 2 tablespoons grated
Garlic powder ½ teaspoon
Tomato sauce 1 cup
Oregano 1 teaspoon
Mushrooms ½ cup sliced (or 1 4-ounce can of stems and pieces)
Sliced olives ½ cup
Green onions 2, thinly sliced
Mozzarella cheese 2 cups shredded
Pepperoni slices or browned and crumbled pork sausage 1 cup

Combine first 6 ingredients; press onto large buttered pizza pan. Bake about 10 minutes at 450°, or until firm and lightly browned. Remove from oven and top with remaining ingredients. Bake about 20 minutes at 350°. Let stand 5 minutes, then slice into wedges and serve. Serves 4.

Italian Skillet

Hot italian sausages 2
Zucchini 4 medium, sliced
Onion 1, coarsely chopped
Tomato sauce 1 8-ounce can
Oregano ½ teaspoon
Garlic salt ½ teaspoon
Sugar ½ teaspoon
Basil ½ teaspoon
Fresh ground pepper ¼ teaspoon
Wheat germ 2 tablespoons

Slice sausage very thin; saute in Teflon* skillet for 10 minutes; set aside. Saute zucchini and onion in same skillet for 5 minutes or until onion is golden. Add tomato sauce and seasonings; sprinkle with wheat germ. Arrange sausage slices on top of mixture; cover and cook for 10 minutes. Serves 4.
* If not using Teflon, add bit of vegetable oil, then drain off oil after all sauteing.

Cornmeal Casserole

Yellow cornmeal 1 cup
Salt 1 teaspoon
Fresh ground pepper ⅛ teaspoon
Onion ½, grated
Water 2¾ cups
Hot italian sausages 2, thinly sliced
Mushrooms ½ pound, sliced
Zucchini 2½ cups sliced
Ripe olives ½ cup sliced
Water 1 cup
Red wine ½ cup
Tomato paste 1 6-ounce can
Dry spaghetti sauce seasoning mix 1 package
Parmesan cheese

Mix cornmeal, salt, pepper, and onion with 1 cup cold water. Stir this into 1¾ cups boiling water. Cook, stirring, until mixture boils; then cook on very low heat for 10 minutes. Pour into buttered 8 × 8-inch pan and chill several hours or overnight. Cut cornmeal into 1-inch squares.

Saute thinly sliced sausage in skillet until browned; pour off excess fat. Add mushrooms and zucchini; saute a few minutes more. Add olives, water, wine, tomato paste, and spaghetti seasoning mix. Simmer 10 minutes. Arrange cornmeal cubes in shallow buttered 2-quart casserole. Cover them with zucchini sauce. Sprinkle with parmesan cheese; bake at 350° for 25 to 30 minutes. Serves 6.

This is good hot, cold, or reheated.

Bacon Zucchini Dinner

Bacon   1 pound, sliced
Onion   1¼ cups chopped
Green pepper   ¾ cup
Garlic clove   1, crushed
Zucchini   3 cups sliced
Ripe olives   1 cup sliced
Sherry or red wine   ¼ cup
Flour   1 tablespoon
Condensed tomato soup   1 10¾-ounce can
Salt   ¼ teaspoon
Chili powder   1 teaspoon
Romano cheese   ¼ cup grated

Cook bacon in skillet until crisp. Drain on paper towel. Pour off most of fat; add chopped onion, green pepper, and garlic. Saute 3 minutes; add zucchini; saute 5 minutes, stirring gently. Stir in half the bacon. Add olives, sherry mixed with flour, tomato soup, and seasonings. Heat through; spoon into oiled casserole. Sprinkle with romano cheese; bake at 350° approximately 20 minutes. Garnish with remaining half of bacon. Serves 6 to 8.

On a tight budget? Make this with ½ pound bacon and skip the garnish. It still tastes delicious.

Fried Spaghetti

Bacon   4 slices, chopped
Eggs   3
Salt   2 teaspoons
Fresh ground pepper   ½ teaspoon
Onion   2 tablespoons grated
Medium cheddar cheese   ½ cup shredded
Spaghetti   8 ounces, cooked and drained
Zucchini   1½ cups thinly sliced
Butter
Parmesan cheese

Fry bacon in large skillet until browned. Beat together eggs, salt, pepper, and onion. Stir in cheese, spaghetti, and zucchini. Scoop bacon up with slotted spoon; mix into spaghetti mixture. Pour mixture into heated skillet with bacon fat; fry until brown. Cut across center; turn both halves; fry until brown. Cut in wedges; spread with butter and sprinkle with parmesan cheese if desired. Serves 6.

Zucchini Quiche

Pie shell   9-inch, unbaked
Margarine   1 tablespoon, softened
Bacon   8 slices
Zucchini   3 cups cubed (can be firm flesh of large one, peeled and center
   pulp discarded)
Eggs   4
Cream or undiluted canned milk   ½ cup
Marjoram   ½ teaspoon
Basil   ½ teaspoon
Onion salt   ¾ teaspoon
Cayenne pepper   dash
Swiss or medium cheddar cheese   (or combination) 2 cups shredded

Spread pie shell with soft margarine, sprinkle with bacon that has been fried crisp, drained on absorbent paper, and crumbled.

Steam zucchini until tender, then drain well. Combine zucchini with eggs in blender container and blend until smooth. Add cream; blend briefly to mix. Stir in seasonings and fold in cheese. Pour into the prepared pie shell. Bake at 425° for 10 minutes, then reduce heat to 300° and bake for 30 to 40 minutes, or until center is set, and a knife inserted halfway between edge and center comes out clean. Let stand 10 minutes before cutting to serve. Serves 6.
Note: These can be made in little foil pie tins for individual servings. In individual pielets, bake at 375° for about 30 to 35 minutes.

Zucchini and Rice Quiche

Bacon 4 slices, chopped, browned, and drained
Zucchini 2 cups thinly sliced
Green onions ½ cup thinly sliced
Bacon drippings 3 tablespoons
Dairy sour cream 1 cup
Seasoning salt 1 teaspoon
Garlic powder ¾ teaspoon
Eggs 6, beaten
Cooked rice 2 cups
Cheddar cheese ⅔ cup shredded
Unbaked pastry shell for 10-inch quiche pan or 9-inch springform pan

Set aside bacon; saute zucchini and onion in bacon drippings until barely tender. Set aside. Stir sour cream and seasonings into eggs, then stir in rice, cheese, and sauteed zucchini. Sprinkle bacon onto pastry shell, then pour in egg mixture. Bake about 45 minutes at 350°, or until set and golden brown. Let stand 5 minutes before cutting. Can be served hot, warm, or cold. Serves 6.

Chicken and Rice Casserole

Zucchini 2 cups coarsely chopped
Onion ½ cup chopped
Butter or margarine 2 tablespoons
Chunk chicken 1 6¾-ounce can (or 1 cup diced leftover chicken)
Cream of chicken soup 1 10¾-ounce can
Cooked rice 2 cups
Cheddar cheese 1½ cups shredded

Saute zucchini and onion in butter; remove from heat. Mix with chicken, soup, and rice. Stir in 1 cup of cheese. Spoon into buttered 1½-quart casserole and sprinkle with remaining cheese. Bake at 350° for about ½ hour. Serves 6.

Chicken with Herbs

Wheat germ   2 tablespoons
Flour   2 tablespoons
Chicken seasoned salt   1 teaspoon
Fryer thighs   8 (or chicken pieces)
Vegetable oil   2 tablespoons
Condensed tomato soup   1 10¾-ounce can
Tomatoes   6, cut in wedges
Zucchini   2 cups sliced
Seasoned salt   1 teaspoon, or less, to taste
Thyme   1 teaspoon
Basil   ½ teaspoon
Imo or yogurt   ½ cup
Noodles   hot buttered

Combine wheat germ, flour, and chicken seasoned salt. Toss chicken parts in this to coat well. Heat oil in large skillet and brown chicken. Add tomato soup; cover and cook on very low heat for 45 minutes, stirring occasionally. Add tomatoes, zucchini, and seasonings. Cover and simmer 15 minutes more, until vegetables are tender. Remove vegetables and chicken to hot serving dish. Stir Imo into sauce in skillet. Reheat, but do not boil. Serve on hot buttered noodles. Serves 4.

Mrs. Pitre's Chicken-Smothered Zucchini

Fryer   1 small, cut up
Salt and pepper   to taste
Vegetable oil   2 tablespoons
Zucchini   2 medium
Chicken liver
Butter   1 tablespoon
Garlic salt   pinch
Fresh tarragon   1 teaspoon chopped
Rice   2 cups cooked and buttered

Cut up fryer; set liver aside. Season fryer to taste; brown in oil in dutch oven. Cover and cook very slowly for 35 minutes. Slice zucchini; add to chicken. Cover again and cook slowly for 10 minutes, stirring carefully from time to time. Saute chopped chicken liver in butter; sprinkle it with garlic salt. Add to chicken; stir gently. Sprinkle with chopped tarragon. Serve on hot buttered rice. Serves 4.

Chicken Liver Casserole

Zucchini   2 cups sliced
Cooked potato   3 cups sliced
Chicken livers   1½ pounds
Butter   3 tablespoons
Pork-and-chicken seasoning salt   1 teaspoon
Fresh ground pepper   ½ teaspoon
Cream   ½ cup
Dairy sour cream   1 cup
Fresh parsley   1 tablespoon chopped

Steam zucchini slices until tender; layer alternately with potato slices in large shallow casserole dish. Saute chicken livers in butter until cooked and golden brown. Season and place on top of vegetables in casserole. Stir cream into pan drippings, then mix in sour cream and pour mixture over chicken livers. Sprinkle with parsley. Bake about 15 minutes at 400°: Serves 4.

Zucchini Combo

Ham   3 slices, cooked and cut in narrow strips
Chicken livers   ½ pound, cut up
Mushrooms   ¼ pound, sliced
Butter or margarine   3 tablespoons
Condensed tomato soup   1 10¾-ounce can
Sherry or red wine   3 tablespoons
Zucchini   3 cups steamed cubes
Romano cheese   ¼ cup grated

Saute ham, livers, and mushrooms in butter. Add tomato soup and sherry; heat but do not boil. Steam zucchini cubes until tender; add to mixture and stir lightly. Sprinkle with grated romano cheese; brown lightly under broiler. Serves 4 to 6.

Zucchini and Shrimp Stir-Fry

Zucchini   2 cups cut in matchlike strips
Celery   1 cup cut in diagonal slices
Green pepper   1, cut in strips
Mushrooms   ½ pound, sliced
Vegetable oil   1 tablespoon
Shrimp   1 4½-ounce can, drained
Jerusalem artichokes*   ("sunchokes")   1 cup peeled and sliced

In a large skillet or wok, saute zucchini, celery, green pepper, and mushrooms in oil, stir-frying for 5 minutes. Add shrimp and artichokes; cover and steam 3 to 5 minutes.

* This is about the only vegetable I know of that grows more easily than zucchini.

Fish Roll-ups

Zucchini 1 cup diced into ½-inch cubes
Eggplant 1 cup peeled and diced
Onion ½ cup chopped
Oil 1 tablespoon
Eggs 2, beaten
Ritz crackers 1 cup crushed
Salt and pepper to taste
Fish fillets 6 (sole or red snapper)

Saute zucchini, eggplant, and onion in oil until tender. Remove from heat; add remaining ingredients (except fish). Divide mixture between fish fillets. Roll fish around mixture; place rolls side by side in oiled casserole. Bake 45 minutes at 325°, or until fish is tender. Serves 6.

Tuna-Stuffed Zucchini Boats

Tuna 2 6½-ounce cans, drained
Ripe olives 1 cup chopped
Soft bread crumbs 1½ cups
Garlic cloves 2, crushed
Parsley 2 tablespoons chopped
Green pepper 1, finely chopped
Eggs 2, beaten
Zucchini 6 medium, cut in half lengthwise
Vegetable oil
White wine

Drain tuna and flake. Add chopped olives, bread crumbs, garlic, parsley, green pepper, and beaten eggs. Steam or boil zucchini for 5 minutes; scoop out the center pulp and seeds and discard, leaving only ¼-inch-thick shell for stuffing. Replace pulp with tuna stuffing, mounded up. Arrange zucchini halves on greased cookie sheet or shallow baking pan. Bake at 350° for about 30 minutes until zucchini is tender, basting occasionally with mixture of equal amounts of oil and white wine. Serves 6.

Pickles and Relishes

Watermelon Pickles

Zucchini   3 pounds, peeled
Alum   4 tablespoons
Water   3 quarts
Ice cubes
Sugar   8 cups
Cinnamon sticks   4
Vinegar   4 cups
Cloves   4 teaspoons
Sugar   1½ cups

Peel and chunk zucchini. Heat alum in 3 quarts water but do not boil. Pour this over zucchini; cover with ice cubes and let stand 2 hours. Drain. Bring remaining ingredients (except 1½ cups sugar) to boil; pour over zucchini and leave overnight. Drain and reheat this syrup 3 mornings, adding an additional ½ cup sugar each time, and pour over zucchini. Red or green food coloring may be added. Boil up, pack into sterilized jars, and seal on the third day.

Bread-and-Butter Pickles

Zucchini   4 quarts chunks or small slices
White onions   6, sliced
Green peppers   2, chopped
Red peppers   2, chopped
Garlic cloves   2
Pickling salt   ½ cup
Cracked ice
Sugar   5 cups
Cider vinegar   3 cups
Turmeric powder   1½ teaspoons
Mustard seed   2 tablespoons
Celery seed   1 teaspoon

Put first 6 ingredients in crock. Put cracked ice over top. Let stand 3 hours. Drain, but do not wash. Bring remaining ingredients to boil; add pickle ingredients; cook about 20 minutes. Pack into sterilized jars and seal.

Dill Pickles

Dill heads   6
Garlic cloves   6
Horseradish root   6 thin slices
Zucchini   5 pounds, cut in chunks (can be firm flesh of very large one)
Water   2 quarts
Vinegar   1 quart
Salt   ⅔ cup
Alum   1 teaspoon

Put 1 head dill, 1 clove garlic, 1 slice horseradish root in each pint jar. Wash and pack zucchini chunks into jars. Boil up water and vinegar; add salt and alum; pour over zucchini chunks in jars and seal. Process in water bath for 5 minutes. These are ready to eat in 6 weeks. Makes approximately 6 pints.

Sandwich Pickles

Zucchini   2 pounds small
Onions   2 small, peeled and sliced
Water
Salt   ¼ cup
White vinegar   2 cups
Pickling spices   3 teaspoons
Turmeric powder   1 teaspoon
Sugar   2 cups

Slice zucchini and onions; cover with water and add salt. Let stand 3 hours. Drain. Combine remaining ingredients; bring to boil. Pour over slices and let stand for 2 hours; then bring syrup and slices to a boil for 5 minutes. Pack in sterilized jars and seal hot.

Christmas Relish

Zucchini 12 cups coarsely ground
Green peppers 2, coarsely ground
Sweet red peppers 2, chopped
Onions 4 cups coarsely ground
Pickling salt ⅓ cup
Turmeric powder 1 teaspoon
Curry powder 1 teaspoon
Celery seed 1 teaspoon
Cornstarch 1 tablespoon
Pepper ½ teaspoon
Vinegar 3 cups
Sugar 4½ cups

In large enamel pan, mix pickling salt into vegetables. Let stand overnight. Drain and rinse with cold water. Mix together rest of ingredients; add to vegetables in large enamel pan; boil 20 minutes. Pour into sterilized jars and seal.

Zucchini Relish

Celery 4 stalks, chopped
Zucchini 10 cups peeled and chopped (can be firm flesh of very large one)
Onions 4 large, chopped
Red pepper 1, chopped
Pickling salt ½ cup
Vinegar 3 cups
Sugar 3¼ cups
Celery seed 2½ teaspoons
Mustard seed 2½ teaspoons
Turmeric powder 2 teaspoons
Cornstarch 2 tablespoons, dissolved in
Vinegar ½ cup

Combine vegetables and pickling salt in large enamel or stainless steel pan; let stand overnight; then drain and rinse well. Bring to boil vinegar, sugar, and seasonings; add chopped vegetables; remove from heat and let stand for 2 hours. Return to stove; bring to boil. Add cornstarch dissolved in vinegar; simmer 15 minutes. Spoon into sterilized jars; seal. Process in water bath for 20 minutes. Makes about 15 half-pints.

Zucchini Fish Sauce (Tartar Sauce)

Zucchini   ½ cup shredded, drained (can be firm flesh of very large one)
Dairy sour cream   ¾ cup
Mayonnaise   ¼ cup
Prepared horseradish   1 tablespoon
Dill pickle   1 tablespoon finely chopped
Chives   1 tablespoon finely chopped
Salt   ¼ teaspoon
White peppercorns   ⅛ teaspoon fresh ground

Mix all together; chill. Serve like tartar sauce with fish.

Sylvia's Zucchini Marmalade

Orange   1, seeded
Maraschino cherries and syrup   1 8-ounce jar
Yellow or green zucchini   5 pounds seeded and peeled (can be from very large ones)
Crushed pineapple and juice   1 20-ounce can
Lemons   juice of 2
Sugar   5 pounds

Slice orange and peeling; chop in blender (or grind). Put in large cooking kettle. Chop cherries in blender (or grind); add to kettle. Chop zucchini in blender—2½ pounds coarsely chopped, 2½ pounds blended quite fine; add all to cooking kettle. Add rest of ingredients; mix together and cook until desired thickness is obtained. Pour into sterilized jars and seal.

Low-Sodium Chutney

Zucchini 6 cups sliced and ground coarsely (use very large zucchini, remove center pulp and seeds, but do not peel)
Green peppers 2, coarsely ground
Tart apples 2 cups, cored but not peeled, coarsely ground
Onion 1, finely ground
Raisins or dates ¾ pound, ground
Celery seed 1 tablespoon
Honey 1 cup
Lemon 1, juice and grated rind
Vinegar 1⅓ cups
Frozen concentrated orange juice ⅓ cup, undiluted

Combine all ingredients and simmer until thick. Spoon into sterilized jars; seal and process in boiling water bath for 10 minutes. Jars to be used soon need not be processed; keep well in refrigerator. This chutney mellows and blends flavors after a week or two.

Note: This really spices up a no-salt diet. Of your garden vegetables, zucchini is lowest in sodium, .06 milligrams per ½ cup zucchini.

Laverne's Quick Chutney

Butter or margarine ¼ cup
Turmeric 1 teaspoon
Cinnamon sticks 2
Powdered coriander 1 teaspoon
Salt ½ teaspoon (optional)
Mustard seed 1 teaspoon
Zucchini 2 cups cut into ½-inch cubes
Brown sugar 1 cup packed
Lemon 1, quartered and thinly sliced
Tomatoes 1 15-ounce can, drained
Crushed pineapple 1 8-ounce can, drained
Chunk pineapple 1 20-ounce can, drained
Vinegar 1 scant cup

Melt butter in heavy frying pan and add seasonings. Saute zucchini, add brown sugar and lemon and cook 2 or 3 minutes, stirring. Add tomatoes, crushed and chunk pineapple, and vinegar. Simmer 5 to 10 minutes, stirring often. Remove cinnamon sticks. Serve hot, or chill in refrigerator. Lasts a long time in the refrigerator.

Soups, Salads,
and Salad Dressing

Vegetable Soup

Soup meat (neck)   1½ pounds
Soup bones   ½ pound, cracked
Onion   1, chopped
Powdered bay leaves   ½ teaspoon
Fresh ground pepper   ¼ teaspoon
Cloves   pinch
Celery leaves   ½ cup chopped
Water   3 quarts cold
Zucchini   3 cups diced—2 cups peeled, 1 cup unpeeled
Onions   1 cup sliced
Carrots   1 cup diced
Celery   1 cup chopped
Potatoes   1 cup diced
Tomatoes   1 28-ounce can
Soup mix grains   ¼ cup
Salt and pepper   to taste

Trim fat off soup meat; cut in ¾-inch cubes. Put soup meat, bones, onion, seasoning, and water in large soup pot. Bring to boil; lower heat and simmer 4 hours, covered. Remove soup bone; skim off fat. Add vegetables and soup mix grains and cook 35 to 45 minutes. Season to taste. Serves 6 to 8.

Cream of Zucchini Soup

Water   2 cups boiling
Chicken bouillon cubes   3
Zucchini   2 cups sliced (can be firm flesh of large one; peel if peeling is tough)
Whole or skim milk   1 cup
Salt and pepper   to taste
Parsley   1 tablespoon minced
Dairy sour cream   4 teaspoons

Dissolve bouillon cubes in boiling water; add zucchini and cook until tender. Whirl in blender until smooth; return to heat. Add milk and season to taste. Heat, but do not boil. Serve hot, sprinkled with chopped parsley and tea-spoon of sour cream. Serves 4.
Note: This can be made in winter, with frozen zucchini slices. They need not be blanched to prepare for freezing, if only to be used in this soup recipe. Just slice into plastic bags, close tops securely, label, and put in freezer. Use later when zucchini is out of season.

Zucchini Milk

Peel, remove, and discard seedy pulp from a very large zucchini. Cut in pieces and feed into vegetable juicer. The pale green liquid that comes out (in profusion) can be used in many ways to add taste and nutrition in cooking—any place where water would ordinarily be used. It can be stored for several days in refrigerator or frozen.

For convenience, freeze juice in ice cube trays. When solidly frozen, remove cubes from trays, and store in plastic bag in freezer. Remove one or two at a time as needed; they melt easily for use in cooking.

Suggested uses: As "water" for cooking other vegetables or for making soups, in gravies or cream sauces, as liquid in Jello for vegetable salad.

Tomatoes Stuffed with Zucchini

Tomatoes   4 large
Zucchini   2 cups shredded (can be firm flesh of very large one)
Salt   1 teaspoon
Salt   ¼ teaspoon
Sugar   ⅛ teaspoon
Fresh ground pepper   ⅛ teaspoon
Garlic clove   1, crushed
Mushrooms   ½ cup sliced
Vegetable oil   1 tablespoon
Mayonnaise   4 teaspoons
Fresh parsley   1 tablespoon minced

Slice off top half inch of tomatoes. Scoop out pulp; chop it and the tops of tomatoes; put in colander to drain. Shred zucchini and sprinkle with teaspoon salt; mix with tomato pulp; leave to drain for ½ hour. Sprinkle inside of tomato shells with mixture of salt, sugar, and pepper. Drain them upside down on paper towels in refrigerator for ½ hour or more. Squeeze zucchini lightly; then saute in Teflon skillet with tomato pulp, garlic, mushrooms, and oil for 5 minutes. Turn up heat and stir constantly until all moisture is evaporated. Season to taste with salt and pepper. Cool mixture; chill for ½ hour or more. Stuff tomato shells and garnish with mayonnaise and parsley. Serves 4.

Two-Tone Zucchini Gelatin

Plain gelatin 1 tablespoon
Cold water ½ cup
Zucchini 1¼ cups cubed (unpeeled if small; peeled and pulp removed, if
large one)
Frozen concentrated apple juice ½ cup, thawed
Green food coloring 2 drops
Frozen concentrated apple juice ½ cup

Soak gelatin in water. Simmer zucchini in ½ cup apple juice until tender.
Blend in blender. Add food coloring. Add soaked gelatin; blend well. Add
frozen apple juice; blend. Add more water, if necessary, to bring total amount
to just under 2 cups. Pour into individual molds or serving glasses. Chill. This
forms 2 layers, one solid dark green, one fluffy pale green. Very pretty.

Potato Zucchini Salad

Salad oil ¼ cup
Potatoes 3 cups cooked and shredded (do not overcook)
Zucchini 1 cup shredded
Onion ½, grated
Garlic powder ¼ teaspoon
Dill seed ½ teaspoon
Seasoned salt 1 teaspoon
Mayonnaise ¼ cup
French dressing ¼ cup

Pour oil over potatoes, add zucchini and onion. Toss lightly. Mix rest of
ingredients, stir carefully into potato mixture. Chill at least 2 hours before
serving. Serves 4.

Bean Zucchini Salad

Zucchini   1½ cups small, thinly sliced
Green pepper   1, cut in strips
Green beans   1 cup cooked (canned or fresh)
Red kidney beans   1 15½-ounce can, drained well
Green onions   3, thinly sliced (or 1 medium onion, sliced and separated
   into rings)
Vinegar   3 tablespoons
Vegetable oil   3 tablespoons
Seasoned salt   1 teaspoon
Sugar   1 teaspoon
Freshly ground pepper   ¼ teaspoon

Combine vegetables. Combine rest of ingredients; pour over vegetables and
stir well. Refrigerate in covered bowl for several hours, stirring occasionally.
Toss lightly before serving. Serves 6.

Summer Supper Salad

Mayonnaise   ¼ cup
French dressing   ¼ cup
Wieners   4, cut in half crosswise, then cut in strips
Peas   ½ cup cooked
Zucchini   1 cup diced
Dill pickle   ¼ cup chopped
Celery   ¼ cup thinly sliced
Carrot   ¼ cup shredded
Salad greens

Mix together mayonnaise and french dressing; add rest of ingredients (except
greens). Mix lightly; chill well. Serve on salad greens. Serves 4.

Hot Dutch Vegetable Salad

Zucchini 2 cups sliced and cooked tender-crisp
Cabbage 2 to 3 cups chopped and cooked tender-crisp
Peas 1 cup, cooked and drained
Celery 1 cup thinly sliced and cooked
Green onions 2, chopped but not cooked
French dressing ½ cup
Imo or dairy sour cream 1 cup
Bacon 4 slices, diced and cooked crisp

Cook first 4 vegetables individually, either by steaming or cooking in small quantity of water until water is almost gone, then draining well. Use a buttered 9 × 13-inch baking pan, or buttered 9 × 12-inch Pyrex pan, preheated. (The preheated Pyrex pan holds the heat well, if taking this dish to potluck.) Layer cooked and drained vegetables in pan, one vegetable at a time. Sprinkle with chopped green onions, then with french dressing. Top with small dabs of Imo or sour cream and garnish with bacon. Hot salad can be served at once, or kept warm in 200° oven for up to ½ hour. Could be made 1 hour or more in advance, kept at room temperature, and then heated in oven just before serving. Serves 8.

Celery Zucchini Salad

Zucchini 1 medium
Celery 3 stalks
Garlic salt 1 teaspoon
Water ice
Plain yogurt 1 cup
Fresh ground white pepper ⅛ teaspoon
Onion salt ½ teaspoon
Salad herbs ¼ teaspoon
Salad greens

Slice zucchini and celery very thin; sprinkle with garlic salt; cover with ice water for 1 hour. Drain in colander and pat dry with paper towels. Mix remaining ingredients (except greens); toss lightly with celery and zucchini. Serve on salad greens. Serves 4 to 6.

Zucchini Dill Salad

Zucchini   4 to 6 small*
Salt   sprinkle
Yogurt   ½ cup
Dairy sour cream   ¼ cup
Fresh dill leaves   2 tablespoons minced
Lemon juice   1 tablespoon
Tarragon leaves   1 teaspoon crushed
Shallots   3, finely minced (or 1 small garlic clove, crushed)
Salt and pepper   to taste
Tomatoes
Lettuce

Halve zucchini lengthwise. Scoop out center seeds and pulp. Slice thinly; sprinkle with salt and drain in colander for ½ hour. Pat slices dry with paper towel. Combine next 7 ingredients and stir into zucchini slices; chill for several hours. Serve on sliced tomatoes and lettuce leaves. Serves 2 to 4.
* Total yield after preparing and slicing zucchini should be approximately 2 cups.

Tuna Vegetable Salad

Zucchini   2 cups small sliced (or small slices of very large one)
Water-pack tuna   1 7-ounce can, drained
Green pepper   ½ cup chopped
Celery   ½ cup thinly sliced
Onion   ½ cup sliced in rings
Cherry tomatoes   1 cup halves
Mayonnaise   ¼ cup
French dressing   ¼ cup
Salad herbs   ¼ teaspoon

Steam zucchini slices 5 minutes; drain on paper towels; chill. Combine tuna with rest of vegetables; add mayonnaise, french dressing, and salad herbs, stirred together. Mix. Add chilled zucchini slices; toss lightly. Chill well. Serves 6.

Italian Salad

Salad macaroni ½ 12-ounce package
Onion 1, chopped
Celery 2 stalks, chopped
Garlic clove 1, crushed
Dairy sour cream 1 cup
Zucchini 1½ cups chopped
Peas ½ cup cooked
Celery ½ cup thinly sliced
Ripe olives ¼ cup sliced
Radishes ¼ cup thinly sliced
Italian herb seasoning ½ teaspoon
French dressing 3 tablespoons (optional)

Cook macaroni until tender, but not soft, in well-salted water with onion, celery, and garlic. Drain. Add remainder of ingredients (except dressing); mix well; chill. Just before serving, stir in 3 tablespoons french dressing (optional). Serves 8.

Apple Zucchini Salad

Zucchini 1 small, thinly sliced
Apples 2, cored and diced
Celery ½ cup chopped
Potatoes 1 cup cooked, peeled, and cubed
Bottled italian dressing 2 tablespoons
Tomato ½ small, peeled, seeded, and cubed
Mayonnaise ¼ cup
Red onion 1 small, thinly sliced into rings
Romaine lettuce

Marinate zucchini, apple, celery, and potatoes in italian dressing about 1 hour in refrigerator. Stir tomato into mayonnaise. Toss marinated mixture and half of onion rings with tomato mayonnaise. Serve on romaine and garnish with remaining onion rings. Serves 6.

Zucchini-and-Herb Dressing

Zucchini   1 medium, peeled and sliced
Chives   ¼ cup cut up
Green pepper   ½, cut up
Tomato   1 large, peeled and sliced
Seasoned salt   1 teaspoon
Parsley   1 tablespoon chopped
Cucumber   1 small, peeled and sliced
Salad herbs   ½ teaspoon
Fresh ground pepper   ¼ teaspoon
Salad oil   2 tablespoons
Lemon juice   1 tablespoon
Vinegar   1 tablespoon

Mix all together in large blender container. Cover and whirl by turning on high speed for a few seconds, switching off several times, until ingredients are well chopped. Makes over 2 cups.

Side Dishes, Sauces, and Stuffings

Creamy Sauce

Celery   2 stalks, thinly sliced
Golden zucchini   1 cup sliced
Green zucchini   1 cup sliced (or 2 cups green only)
Milk   ¼ cup
Cream cheese   1 3-ounce package, softened and cubed
Flour   1 tablespoon
Salt and pepper   to taste
Soft bread crumbs   3 tablespoons, sauteed in
Butter   1 tablespoon

Steam celery for 5 minutes; add zucchini slices and steam until zucchini is barely tender. In the meantime, put milk, cream cheese, and flour in blender; whirl until smooth. Combine with vegetables in Teflon saucepan. Cook over low heat, stirring gently, until sauce thickens and boils. Season to taste. Serve topped with buttered crumbs. Serves 4 as side dish.
Note: If you raise your own zucchini, try some of the new hybrid, Golden zucchini, from Burpees. Not much difference in taste, but a wonderful very bright yellow color which adds a different look when combined with regular color zucchini.

Green Zucchini Enchilada Sauce

Zucchini   3 medium or 1 large, quartered, centers and seeds removed
Green tomatoes   6 large, quartered
Onions   1 cup sliced
Garlic cloves   4, crushed
Chicken bouillon cubes   3
Hot water   1 cup
Sugar   ½ teaspoon
Cumin   ½ teaspoon
Green chilies   1 3-ounce can, diced

Put all ingredients, except green chilies, into blender container, a portion at a time. Blend briefly to puree. Add green chilies to puree and simmer in sauce-pan for 30 to 40 minutes, until sauce thickens. This may be used fresh, or frozen for later use. Makes enough sauce for 4 to 6 enchiladas.

Zucchini with Bacon

Zucchini 6 about 6-inch length, or 4 about 8-inch length
Bacon 6 slices, crisply fried and crumbled
Bacon drippings 3 tablespoons
Vinegar 2 tablespoons
Sugar 2 teaspoons
Seasoning salt ½ teaspoon
Flour 2 tablespoons

Slice zucchini thinly into saucepan. Add bacon, drippings, vinegar, sugar, and seasoning. Simmer, covered, until tender. Sift flour onto zucchini and cook, stirring, for a few minutes until consistency of thick gravy. Serves 4.

Zucchini a la Di Julio

Bacon 2 strips, cut in 1-inch pieces
Zucchini 3 small, about 1 inch in diameter
Onion ½ medium
Stewed tomatoes or tomato sauce 3 tablespoons
Salt and pepper to taste

Saute bacon until lightly browned; drain excess fat. Cut zucchini into ¼-inch slices; slice onion; mix with zucchini and add to bacon. Add tomatoes, salt and pepper to taste. Cover skillet and steam for 20 minutes or until done.

Zucchini in Agrodolce

Zucchini 6 large, trimmed and cut into quarters lengthwise
Olive oil 2½ tablespoons
Garlic clove 1, crushed
Wine vinegar 2½ tablespoons
Water 2½ tablespoons
Pine nuts 2 to 3 tablespoons
Seedless white raisins 2 to 3 tablespoons
Salted anchovies (italian) 2, chopped
Salt

Prepare zucchini. Heat oil in large skillet; saute garlic and discard. Add zucchini; cover pan and cook a few minutes. Add vinegar and water; cook over moderate heat 10 minutes. Add nuts, raisins, and washed and chopped anchovies. Salt to taste. Cook 2 to 3 minutes longer.

Saucy Zucchini

Vegetable oil   1 tablespoon
Onion   1, finely chopped
Garlic clove   1, crushed or minced
Zucchini   2 medium, cut in ¼-inch slices
Salt   ¼ teaspoon
Fresh ground pepper   ⅛ teaspoon
Dried marjoram   ¼ teaspoon
Tomato sauce   1 8-ounce can
Egg   1, hard-cooked, chopped
Parsley   1 tablespoon chopped
Onion salt   ¼ teaspoon

Saute onion and garlic in oil until onion is golden. Add zucchini slices and seasoning; saute a few minutes longer. Cover with tomato sauce and simmer slowly until zucchini is barely tender. Serve garnished with mixture of egg, parsley, and onion salt. Serves 4.

India Fried Zucchini

Flour   ½ cup
Baking powder   ¾ teaspoon
Salt   ½ teaspoon
Turmeric   ½ teaspoon
Curry powder   1 teaspoon (or more, to taste)
Milk   ½ cup
Egg   1
Zucchini   1 medium, cut in ¼-inch slices
Oil   for frying

Beat first 7 ingredients together. Dip zucchini slices in batter; fry in hot oil until golden brown, turning once. Drain on paper towel, if necessary, then salt to taste. (These may be kept warm and crisp in 300° oven until all are fried and ready to serve.) Serves 4 to 6.

Summer Favorite

Water ½ cup
Chicken bouillon 1 cube
Onion 1 small, sliced and separated into rings
Tomatoes 2 large or 3 small, quartered
Frozen peas ½ 10-ounce package, thawed (or 1 cup fresh)
Zucchini 2 cups sliced
Flour 1 tablespoon
Basil pinch
Seasoned salt

Dissolve bouillon cube in boiling water; add onion, tomatoes, and peas. Cover; simmer gently 5 minutes. Add zucchini; simmer until zucchini is barely tender. Remove vegetables from liquid with slotted spoon; keep warm. Pour off ¼ cup of liquid, cool in measuring cup, and blend in 1 tablespoon flour; return to saucepan with hot liquid; simmer until thickened. Season to taste; add vegetables and reheat. Serves 4.

Breakfast Scrambled Eggs in Zucchini Shells

Zucchini 4 small, about 8-inch length
Cooking oil 2 tablespoons
Eggs 6, beaten
Catsup ½ cup
Garlic clove 1, crushed
Salt and pepper to taste
Parmesan cheese ¼ cup grated

Cut zucchini in half lengthwise. Steam to soften, then saute halves gently in oil. Scoop out centers. Dice ½ cup of pulp and saute in same oil until tender; then add eggs, catsup, garlic, salt, and pepper. Stir, scrambling until just set. Spoon mixture into zucchini shells. Put shells onto oiled cookie sheet and sprinkle with parmesan. Bake about 10 minutes at 400°. Serves 4.

Orange Zucchini

Zucchini   4 cups sliced
Salt
Margarine or butter   1 tablespoon, melted
Mandarin orange sections   1 11-ounce can
Cornstarch   2 teaspoons
Nutmeg   ¼ teaspoon
Slivered almonds   4 tablespoons

Steam zucchini slices until barely tender. Remove to pan and salt lightly. Add melted margarine; set aside and keep warm. Pour syrup from orange sections; blend cornstarch into syrup and simmer until thickened and clear. Add nutmeg. Add orange sections and reheat. Pour over warm zucchini slices and sprinkle with slivered almonds. Serves 4 to 6.

Chinese Zucchini

Vegetable oil   1 teaspoon
Celery   1 cup thinly sliced
Pod peas   ½ pound
Mushrooms   ½ cup sliced
Zucchini   2 cups thinly sliced
Bean sprouts   ½ pound
Soy sauce

In Teflon skillet or wok, cook celery in oil over medium heat, stirring, for several minutes. Add pod peas, mushrooms, and zucchini. Cook, stirring, for several minutes. Add bean sprouts; stir and cook until bean sprouts are very lightly cooked. Serve with soy sauce. Serves 4 to 6.

Sweet-and-Sour Zucchini

Zucchini   4 small, sliced
Frozen apple juice   ⅛ cup, undiluted
Cider vinegar   ⅛ cup
Garlic clove   1, crushed
Dill weed   ½ teaspoon

Combine ingredients. Simmer 5 minutes or until zucchini is barely tender, stirring occasionally. Serves 4.

Zucchini Uno Momento

Zucchini   2 cups sliced
Vegetable oil   1 tablespoon
Mushrooms   1 4-ounce can sliced (or stems and pieces)
Flour   1½ tablespoons
Red wine   ½ cup
Oregano   ¼ teaspoon
Thyme   ¼ teaspoon
Salt   to taste
Parsley   1 teaspoon chopped

Saute zucchini in oil until barely tender. While it is cooking, prepare sauce. Drain mushrooms; reserve liquid. Blend flour with mushroom liquid. Cook in small saucepan with wine until thickened, stirring constantly. Add seasonings, then mushrooms and zucchini. Simmer for a few minutes to blend flavors. Sprinkle with parsley. Serves 4.

Chicken-Fried Zucchini

Zucchini   1 medium
Milk   1½ cups (can be canned milk, even sour canned milk, skim, or
  buttermilk)
Vegetable oil   ¼ cup
Cornmeal   ½ cup
Flour   ½ cup
Seasoning salt   1 teaspoon

Slice zucchini in ⅜-inch rounds; soak in milk for ½ hour or more. Heat oil in Teflon skillet on medium heat. Lift zucchini slices out of milk; dip both sides of each slice in breading mixture of cornmeal, flour, and seasoning salt (chicken type seasoning is great in this). Place slices in hot oil and fry until golden; turn and repeat. Do not overcook. Serves 2.
Note: If you have no cornmeal, use cornmeal muffin mix instead of the cornmeal and flour mixture, with added seasoning. Save the milk used for soaking to use in gravies and cream sauces.

Zucchini Fritters

Zucchini   4 7½-inch, peeled
Sourdough french bread   12 slices
Milk
Garlic cloves   4 medium, pressed
Thyme   2 teaspoons
Salt   1½ teaspoons
Pepper   ½ teaspoon
Parmesan cheese   2 cups grated
Eggs   3, beaten
Fine bread crumbs   1½ to 2 cups
Olive oil

Cut zucchini in half; boil in water until tender. Drain and immediately place in bowl to save exuding juices. When cool, place zucchini in suitable pan and mash thoroughly. Pour vegetable juices over 1 or 2 slices bread, squeeze as dry as possible, and crumble bread into mashed zucchini; continue with vegetable juices until juices are used up, then use small amounts of milk to finish soaking and crumbling rest of bread slices.

Add rest of ingredients except bread crumbs and oil; mix thoroughly and slowly add crumbs, mixing well until consistency is suitable for dropping into fry pan for cooking. (Use only sufficient crumbs to achieve a delicate mixture.) Drop by rounded tablespoons into moderately hot fry pan with olive oil; flatten to about ⅔-inch thickness, brown on both sides and serve.

Zucchini a la Stella

Zucchini   1 pound, cut into 1-inch slices
Tomato sauce   1 8-ounce can
Onion   1, sliced
Green pepper   ¼ cup chopped
Ground nutmeg   ¼ teaspoon
Sugar   ¼ teaspoon
Bay leaf   1 crumbled
Salt   ½ teaspoon
Pepper   ½ teaspoon

Mix ingredients in skillet. Simmer until tender, about 20 minutes. Serves 4.

Cookout Zucchini–Skewered

Zucchini 2 medium
Mushrooms ½ pound
Green pepper 1, cut in wedges
Cherry tomatoes 1 basket
Margarine melted
Hot barbecue sauce
Salt and pepper to taste

Slice zucchini in ½-inch rounds; thread on skewers alternating with mushrooms, green pepper, and tomatoes, being careful to skewer zucchini slices horizontally to keep them firmly in place. Brush with margarine and place on barbecue grill over medium hot coals. Turn occasionally, basting with sauce, for about 15 to 20 minutes. Serves 4 to 6.

Cookout Zucchini–In Foil

Tomatoes 4, sliced
Zucchini 2 medium, sliced
Onions 2 large, thinly sliced
Chicken bouillon 1 cube per packet
Fresh ground pepper

Layer several slices of tomato, zucchini, and onion in center of heavy aluminum foil squares. Sprinkle each packet with 1 crushed bouillon cube and pepper. Fold each foil packet and seal with double folds. Place on barbecue grill over medium hot coals; cook 35 to 40 minutes. Serves 6 to 8.

Braised Peas and Zucchini

Zucchini   2 medium, diced (or 3 to 4 cups diced from large zucchini)
Frozen peas   1 10-ounce package, thawed
Margarine   2 tablespoons
Chicken bouillon   1 cube, dissolved in
Water   2 tablespoons hot
Salt and pepper   to taste
Chives   1 teaspoon chopped
Parsley   1 teaspoon chopped

In large Teflon* skillet, saute zucchini and peas in margarine for 5 minutes.
Add bouillon cube and water; season as necessary. Cover tightly and cook 3
to 5 minutes until vegetables are barely tender. Stir in chives and parsley.
Serves 6.
* If not using Teflon, stir often so as not to scorch.

Zucchini with Peppers

Butter or margarine   1 tablespoon
Stale bread   2 slices, cubed
Sweet red pepper   1, cut in strips
Green pepper   1, cut in strips
Celery   ½ cup thinly sliced
Onion   1 small, chopped
Vegetable oil   ¼ cup
Zucchini   3 cups sliced
Garlic salt   1 teaspoon
Fresh ground pepper   ¼ teaspoon
Parmesan cheese   ¼ cup grated
Medium cheddar cheese   ¼ cup shredded

Melt butter in heavy dutch oven; stir in stale bread cubes and saute a few
minutes. Remove bread and set aside. Add red and green peppers, celery,
onion, and oil; saute until onion is golden. Add sliced zucchini, garlic salt,
and pepper. Cover; cook very slowly for 15 minutes or until zucchini is
tender, stirring occasionally. Sprinkle bread cubes over vegetables. Combine
parmesan and cheddar cheeses; sprinkle on top; then put uncovered under
broiler until bread cubes are browned and cheese is melted. Serves 4 to 6.

Ratatouille

Eggplant   1, peeled and cubed
Olive oil   2 tablespoons
Garlic cloves   3, crushed
Vegetable oil   ½ cup
Zucchini   3 cups sliced (can be from very large one)
Onions   3, sliced
Green peppers   2, cut in strips
Tomatoes   5, peeled and chopped
Celery   2 stalks, sliced
Parsley   2 tablespoons minced
Salt   1 teaspoon, or to taste
Fresh ground pepper
Thyme   ½ teaspoon crushed
Marjoram   ¼ teaspoon

In heavy skillet saute eggplant in olive oil until light brown. Put eggplant with garlic in large pot or dutch oven. Add some of vegetable oil to skillet; saute zucchini; remove to pot. Repeat this with onion, green peppers, tomatoes, and celery, adding a little more oil for each vegetable. Add seasonings to pot and cook mixture, stirring, for about 10 minutes; then turn heat very low, cover pot, and simmer slowly for about an hour. If there is any liquid left in pot, uncover and cook it down. This is delicious hot or cold, a good accompaniment for roasts or as filling for omelets. Serves 6 to 8.

This mixture freezes very well. Make it in big batches in late summer when these vegetables are plentiful. Add leftover meats to this for an easy main dish.

Bacon and Zucchini Crunch

Bacon   4 slices
Stale bread   3 slices, cubed
Onion   1 medium, finely chopped
Zucchini   4 cups sliced
Vinegar   2 tablespoons
Frozen apple juice   2 tablespoons, undiluted
Seasoned salt   1 teaspoon

In skillet, cook bacon crisp; remove and keep warm. Pour off and reserve all but 2 tablespoons of the bacon fat. Toast bread, cube, and saute bread cubes in this fat until brown; remove and keep cubes hot. Return 2 tablespoons of reserved fat to skillet. Saute onions and zucchini, stirring gently, until zucchini is barely tender-crisp. Add vinegar, apple juice, and salt. Simmer a few minutes, stirring occasionally. Crumble hot bacon; add bacon and bread cubes to zucchini, stir in, and serve at once. Serves 4 to 6.

Easy Skillet Zucchini

Carrots   2, thinly sliced
Vegetable oil   3 tablespoons
Onion   2 cups sliced in rings
Zucchini   2 medium, thinly sliced
Salt and pepper   to taste
Garlic powder

Saute carrots in oil for 10 minutes. Add onion rings and zucchini slices; season with salt, pepper, and garlic powder. Saute very slowly about 10 minutes, until tender. Serves 4 as side dish.

Jiffy Zucchini in Cheese Sauce

Zucchini   3 cups cubed (can be solid flesh from very large one)
Milk   1 cup
Cornstarch   1 tablespoon
Seasoning salt   1 teaspoon
Dry mustard   ⅓ teaspoon
Cooking sherry or red wine   3 tablespoons
Good melting cheese   3 ounces

Cook zucchini in ½ cup milk in Teflon pan until barely tender. Remove with slotted spoon and keep warm. Stir cornstarch in ½ cup cold milk; add to hot milk in saucepan with seasoning salt, mustard, and wine. Cook, stirring constantly, until thickened. Add zucchini; heat, but do not boil. Add cheese, cut in chunks, and stir only until melted. Serve at once. Serves 4.

Green Zucchini

Zucchini 2 cups cubed (can be firm flesh of very large one)
Italian salad dressing ½ cup
Parsley 1 small bunch
Garlic clove 1, crushed
Soft bread crumbs ¼ cup
Dill pickle ½, sliced

Simmer zucchini cubes in italian dressing until barely tender. Drain dressing off into blender container; add remaining ingredients; whirl together. Pour this sauce over zucchini in saucepan; reheat and serve at once. Serves 4 as side dish.

Matchsticks in Sour Cream

Zucchini 4 cups cut in julienne strips (can be firm flesh of very large one)
Salt 1 teaspoon
Paprika ½ teaspoon
Onion 1, minced
Vegetable oil 4 tablespoons
Flour 1½ tablespoons
Dairy sour cream 1½ cups

Sprinkle zucchini strips with salt; let stand for ½ hour. Drain and pat dry with paper towel. Sprinkle with paprika; cook with onion in hot oil until barely tender. Drain off oil. In the meantime, stir flour into sour cream and simmer until it thickens. Add zucchini; simmer a few minutes longer, stirring gently. Serves 6.

Bean and Zucchini Medley

Onion   1 small, chopped
Vegetable oil   1 tablespoon
Fresh green beans   ½ pound, thinly sliced
Water   1 tablespoon
Zucchini   3 small, sliced
Parsley   1 tablespoon chopped
Thyme   pinch
Salt and pepper   to taste

Cook onions in oil until golden. Add beans and water; steam 5 minutes, covered. Add rest of ingredients, cover, and steam 5 minutes or until vegetables are barely tender. Serves 4.

Zucchini Marinara

Garlic cloves   2, crushed
Olive oil   1 tablespoon
Anchovies   6, minced
Tomatoes   2½ cups canned, mashed
Oregano   ½ teaspoon
Parsley   2 tablespoons chopped
Zucchini   4 cups sliced
Ripe olives   sliced

In saucepan, saute garlic in oil. Add anchovies, tomatoes, oregano, and parsley; simmer 20 minutes, stirring occasionally. Add zucchini slices; simmer until barely tender, stirring gently. Garnish with sliced ripe olives. Serves 6 to 8 as side dish.

Curried Zucchini

Zucchini 3 medium, cubed (can be firm flesh from very large one)
Vegetable oil 1 tablespoon
Garlic clove 1, crushed
Raisins 2 tablespoons
Margarine 2 tablespoons
Flour 2 tablespoons
Water 1 cup
Chicken bouillon 1 cube, crushed
Curry powder ½ teaspoon (or more to taste)
Salt
Unsweetened coconut ¼ cup chopped

Cube zucchini into Teflon pan; saute in oil with garlic and raisins until barely tender. Remove zucchini to warm dish. Melt margarine in same pan; stir in flour. Add water and bouillon cube; stir until sauce becomes thick. Add curry powder and salt; stir. Add zucchini; simmer a minute before serving. Garnish with coconut. Serves 4 as side dish.

Zucchini Patties

Zucchini 2 cups shredded (can be from large one)
Onion 1
Egg 1, slightly beaten
Wheat germ 2 tablespoons
Salt and pepper to taste
Tarragon leaves ½ teaspoon crushed
Flour 2 or 3 tablespoons
Vegetable oil 3 tablespoons
Seasoned salt

Shred zucchini coarsely; drain in colander. Grate onion coarsely. Combine all ingredients except oil and seasoned salt. Use only enough flour to hold mixture together. Heat oil in large Teflon skillet (you may need more oil if not using Teflon). Drop fritter mixture, a tablespoon at a time, into oil. Flatten with back of a spoon. Cook over medium heat until crisp brown; turn and brown on other side. Drain on paper towels; sprinkle with seasoned salt. Can be reheated. Serves 4.

These are delicious, actually taste "meaty" without meat.

Sesame Zucchini

Sesame seeds   2 tablespoons
Vegetable oil   2 tablespoons
Lemon juice   1 teaspoon
Salt   ¼ teaspoon
Hot pepper sauce   ½ teaspoon
Zucchini   2 cups cubed small (can be firm flesh of very large one)
Parsley   chopped

Brown sesame seeds in oil; add rest of seasonings and zucchini. Stir-fry until zucchini is tender-crisp. Garnish with parsley. Serves 4.

Shredded Zucchini Quickie

Zucchini   3 cups shredded, using firm flesh of very large one
Butter or margarine   1 tablespoon, melted
Dairy sour cream   ¾ to 1 cup (or plain yogurt)
Dried tarragon leaves   ½ teaspoon crushed
Salt and pepper   to taste

Remove and discard center pulp and seeds of zucchini; shred firm flesh, about 3 cups, into saucepan. Let stand awhile to bring out juice. Add melted butter; saute, stirring, for about 5 minutes. Drain. Stir in sour cream and tarragon; season to taste. Heat to piping hot, but do not boil. Can be kept warm in oven if necessary. Serves 6.

This is just another way to use up that whopping big zucchini.

Cheese Custard with Zucchini

Zucchini   4 cups unpeeled and shredded
Seasoned salt   1 teaspoon
Flour   ¼ cup
Wheat germ   1 tablespoon
Baking powder   ¼ teaspoon
Medium cheddar cheese   1 cup shredded
Freshly ground pepper   pinch
Chives   2 tablespoons chopped
Parsley   2 tablespoons chopped
Eggs   3
Bacon   4 slices
Margarine   2 tablespoons, softened
Paprika

Toss zucchini with salt, drain in colander for ½ hour, then press as dry as possible. Combine flour, wheat germ, baking powder, cheese, and pepper. Stir into zucchini. Mix in chives, parsley, and lightly beaten eggs. Fry bacon until crisp; crumble. Spread 10-inch shallow casserole with soft margarine; press crumbled bacon on bottom of casserole. Pour in zucchini mixture. Sprinkle with paprika. Bake at 350° for about 25 minutes, or at 325° for 30 minutes, until it tests done in the middle.

Easy Stuffings

Start with medium-size zucchini; count ½ zucchini per person if used as a side dish, or 2 halves per person if it is a meat-stuffed main dish.

Steam or parboil zucchini halves until barely tender if for broiling or less-than-tender if for baking. Scoop out center pulp; either discard it or mix with stuffing.

Bacon and Tomato Squashwich

Tomatoes
Bacon   sliced
Yellow cheese   sliced

Slice tomatoes; cut each slice in half. Fry bacon slices until brown on 1 side only. Fill centers of scooped-out steamed zucchini with tomato half-slices and narrow slices of yellow cheese. Top with slices of bacon, browned side down. Broil to brown top side of bacon.

Mushroom Stuffing

Mushrooms   ½ pound, sliced
Butter   2 tablespoons, melted
Soft bread crumbs   ½ cup
Medium cheddar cheese   ½ cup shredded
Seasoned salt   1 teaspoon

Saute mushrooms in butter; stir in bread crumbs. Add cheese and salt; mix well. Pile steamed centers full of stuffing. Broil just until cheese is melted and tops are lightly browned.

Spinach Stuffing

Milk   ½ cup cold
Flour   2 tablespoons
Frozen chopped spinach   1 10-ounce package, cooked and drained
Bacon   6 slices, cooked crisp and crumbled
Salt and pepper   to taste
Medium cheddar cheese   ¼ cup shredded

In Teflon saucepan, combine milk and flour; heat until it starts to thicken. Add drained cooked spinach; simmer 5 minutes. Add crumbled bacon; season to taste with salt and pepper. Fill steamed halves of 3 medium zucchini; top with cheese. Place on greased cookie sheet and bake at 350° for 15 minutes. If desired, crumbled bacon can be used as topping with cheese.

Mildly Cheese Stuffing

Onion   ¼ cup chopped
Margarine   2 tablespoons
Medium cheddar cheese   ¾ cup shredded
Salt   1 teaspoon
Poultry seasoning   ½ teaspoon
Fresh ground pepper   ⅛ teaspoon
Zucchini pulp   half of what was removed from shells, chopped

Saute onion in margarine. Mix in remaining ingredients. Bake in steamed zucchini shells at 350° for ½ hour.

Bread Stuffing

Soft bread crumbs 3 cups
Onion 1 small, minced
Parsley 1 tablespoon chopped
Eggs 2, beaten
Poultry seasoning ½ teaspoon
Sage ¼ teaspoon
Salt and pepper to taste

Mix ingredients together; fill steamed halves of 3 medium zucchini. Place on oiled cookie sheet and bake at 350° for 30 minutes. Good with turkey roast or chicken. Serves 6.

Beef Stuffing

Ground beef ½ pound
Onion 1, chopped
Tomatoes 1 cup, drained
Dill pickle ¼ cup chopped
Garlic clove 1, crushed
Condensed cream of mushroom soup ½ 10¾-ounce can
Paprika optional

Saute beef and onion until beef is brown and crumbly. Add rest of ingredients. Heat all together; then fill centers. Bake at 350° for 20 minutes. For browned top, sprinkle generously with paprika.

Dieter's Special Stuffing

Seasoned salt
Low-fat cheese

Scoop out shallow indentation in zucchini halves; sprinkle well with seasoned salt; top with pieces of low-fat cheese. Broil long enough to melt cheese and make it bubbly.

Almond Stuffing

Zucchini pulp
Crumbs buttered
Soy sauce   to moisten
Slivered almonds
Butter
Paprika

Mix ingredients together. Stuff centers; dot with butter; sprinkle well with paprika. Bake at 350° for 20 minutes. (This one could also be broiled.)

Beer-Battered Blossoms

Flour   5 tablespoons
Beer   ½ cup
Zucchini blossoms   12
Vegetable oil
Seasoned salt

Mix flour and beer to make batter. Dip zucchini blossoms to coat with batter; fry in oil until golden brown; turn and brown other side. Drain on paper towels. Sprinkle with seasoned salt; serve hot. Serves 4.
Note: You can use quite a few of the male blossoms; just leave enough for good pollination. This is a good treat to fix when frost is predicted—harvest them before the frost kills them.

This easy batter can also be used for frying zucchini slices.

U.S. and Metric Measurements

Approximate conversion formulas are given below for commonly used U.S. and metric kitchen measurements.

Teaspoons	×	5	= milliliters
Tablespoons	×	15	= milliliters
Fluid ounces	×	30	= milliliters
Fluid ounces	×	0.03	= liters
Cups	×	240	= milliliters
Cups	×	0.24	= liters
Pints	×	0.47	= liters
Dry pints	×	0.55	= liters
Quarts	×	0.95	= liters
Dry quarts	×	1.1	= liters
Gallons	×	3.8	= liters
Ounces	×	28	= grams
Ounces	×	0.028	= kilograms
Pounds	×	454	= grams
Pounds	×	0.45	= kilograms
Milliliters	×	0.2	= teaspoons
Milliliters	×	0.07	= tablespoons
Milliliters	×	0.034	= fluid ounces
Milliliters	×	0.004	= cups
Liters	×	34	= fluid ounces
Liters	×	4.2	= cups
Liters	×	2.1	= pints
Liters	×	1.82	= dry pints
Liters	×	1.06	= quarts
Liters	×	0.91	= dry quarts
Liters	×	0.26	= gallons
Grams	×	0.035	= ounces
Grams	×	0.002	= pounds
Kilograms	×	35	= ounces
Kilograms	×	2.2	= pounds

Temperature Equivalents

Fahrenheit	− 32	× 5	÷ 9	= Celsius
Celsius	× 9	÷ 5	+ 32	= Fahrenheit

U.S. Equivalents

1 teaspoon	= ⅓ tablespoon
1 tablespoon	= 3 teaspoons
2 tablespoons	= 1 fluid ounce
4 tablespoons	= ¼ cup or 2 ounces
5⅓ tablespoons	= ⅓ cup or 2⅔ ounces
8 tablespoons	= ½ cup or 4 ounces
16 tablespoons	= 1 cup or 8 ounces
⅜ cup	= ¼ cup plus 2 tablespoons
⅝ cup	= ½ cup plus 2 tablespoons
⅞ cup	= ¾ cup plus 2 tablespoons
1 cup	= ½ pint or 8 fluid ounces
2 cups	= 1 pint or 16 fluid ounces
1 liquid quart	= 2 pints or 4 cups
1 liquid gallon	= 4 quarts

Metric Equivalents

1 milliliter	= 0.001 liter
1 liter	= 1000 milliliters
1 milligram	= 0.001 gram
1 gram	= 1000 milligrams
1 kilogram	= 1000 grams

Index

Other Books from Pacific Search Press

COOKING

American Wood Heat Cookery (2d Ed. Revised & Enlarged) by Margaret
    Byrd Adams
The Apple Cookbook by Kyle D. Fulwiler
The Bean Cookbook: Dry Legume Cookery by Norma S. Upson
The Berry Cookbook (2d Ed. Revised & Enlarged) by Kyle D. Fulwiler
Canning and Preserving without Sugar (Updated) by Norma M.
    MacRae, R.D.
The Eating Well Cookbook by John Doerper
Eating Well: A Guide to Foods of the Pacific Northwest by John Doerper
The Eggplant Cookbook by Norma S. Upson
A Fish Feast by Charlotte Wright
Food 101: A Student Guide to Quick and Easy Cooking by Cathy Smith
One Potato, Two Potato: A Cookbook by Constance Bollen and
    Marlene Blessing
River Runners' Recipes by Patricia Chambers
The Salmon Cookbook by Jerry Dennon
Shellfish Cookery: Absolutely Delicious Recipes from the West Coast
    by John Doerper
Starchild & Holahan's Seafood Cookbook by Adam Starchild and
    James Holahan
Wild Mushroom Recipes by Puget Sound Mycological Society

CRAFTS

The Chilkat Dancing Blanket by Cheryl Samuel
The Guide to Successful Tapestry Weaving by Nancy Harvey
An Illustrated Guide to Making Oriental Rugs by Gordon W. Scott
Patterns for Tapestry Weaving: Projects and Techniques by Nancy Harvey
Spinning and Weaving with Wool (Updated) by Paula Simmons

HEALTH

A Practical Guide to Independent Living for Older People by Alice H.
    Phillips and Caryl K. Roman

NATURE

The Birdhouse Book: Building Houses, Feeders, and Baths by Don McNeil
Growing Organic Vegetables West of the Cascades by Steve Solomon
Marine Mammals of Eastern North Pacific and Arctic Waters edited by
    Delphine Haley
Seabirds of Eastern North Pacific and Arctic Waters edited by
  Delphine Haley

NORTHWEST SCENE

At the Forest's Edge: Memoir of a Physician-Naturalist by
David Tirrell Hellyer
The Pike Place Market: People, Politics, and Produce by Alice Shorett
and Murray Morgan
Seattle Photography by David Barnes
They Tried to Cut It All by Edwin Van Syckle

OUTDOOR RECREATION

Cross-Country Downhill and Other Nordic Mountain Skiing Techniques
(3d Ed. Revised & Enlarged) by Steve Barnett
The Coastal Kayaker: Kayak Camping on the Alaska and B.C. Coast by
Randel Washburne
Derek C. Hutchinson's Guide to Sea Kayaking by Derek C. Hutchinson
Kayak Trips in Puget Sound and the San Juan Islands by Randel
Washburne
River Runners' Recipes by Patricia Chambers
*The White-Water River Book: A Guide to Techniques, Equipment,
Camping, and Safety* by Ron Watters / Robert Winslow, photography
*Whitewater Trips for Kayakers, Canoeists and Rafters in British
Columbia, Greater Vancouver through Whistler and Thompson River
Regions* by Betty Pratt-Johnson
*Whitewater Trips for Kayakers, Canoeists and Rafters on Vancouver
Island* by Betty Pratt-Johnson

TRAVEL

Alaska's Backcountry Hideaways: Southcentral by Roberta L. Graham
Alaska's Southeast: Touring the Inside Passage (2d Ed. Revised &
Enlarged) by Sarah Eppenbach
Cruising the Columbia and Snake Rivers (2d Ed. Revised & Enlarged) by
Sharlene P. and Ted W. Nelson and Joan LeMieux
Cruising the Pacific Coast, Acapulco to Skagway (4th Ed. Revised) by
Carolyn and Jack West
The Getaway Guide I: Short Vacations in the Pacific Northwest (2d Ed.
Revised & Enlarged) by Marni and Jake Rankin
The Getaway Guide II: More Short Vacations in the Pacific Northwest
(2d Ed. Revised & Enlarged) by Marni and Jake Rankin
The Getaway Guide III: Short Vacations in Northern California by Marni
and Jake Rankin
The Getaway Guide IV: Short Vacations in Southern California by
Marni and Jake Rankin
Journey to the High Southwest: A Traveler's Guide (2d Ed. Revised)
by Robert Casey